Wonderful ways to prepare

BARBECUE
& PICNIC MEALS

by MARION MANSFIELD

SCALLOP KEBABS WITH WHITE BUTTER SAUCE (RECIPE PAGE 24)

Wonderful ways to prepare

BARBECUE
& PICNIC MEALS

H.C. PUBLISHING INC.
FLORIDA, USA

COVER PICTURE — BARBECUED STEAK, CHOPS AND SAUSAGES (RECIPE PAGE 21)

FIRST PUBLISHED 1979
REPRINTED 1984
FIRST US EDITION 1984

PUBLISHED AND COPYRIGHT © 1979
BY AYERS & JAMES
CROWS NEST, N.S.W., AUSTRALIA

DISTRIBUTED BY
AYERS & JAMES, CROWS NEST, N.S.W., AUSTRALIA
H.C. PUBLISHING INC., U.S.A.

PRINTED IN SINGAPORE

HARD COVER EDITION: ISBN 0 87637 926 9
SOFT COVER EDITION: ISBN 0 87637 938 2

TITLES AVAILABLE IN THIS SERIES: BEEF,
FISH & SEAFOOD, POULTRY, STEWS & CASSEROLES,
BARBECUES & PICNIC MEALS, CHINESE MEALS,
SALADS, SOUPS, ITALIAN MEALS, LAMB,
CAKES & COOKIES, DESSERTS.

◄ OVERLEAF — PICNIC MENU (RECIPES PAGES 80–82)   PATIO PICNIC (RECIPE PAGE 21) ►

Kebabs of Veal Liver and Ham

Serves: 5
Cooking time: 20−25 minutes
Barbecue on skewers over hot coals

¾ lb (375 g) calves liver
¾ lb (375 g) thick cut ham steak
1 lb (500 g) medium size mushrooms
2 medium green bell peppers
¾ lb (375 g) cooked ribbon noodles
5 tablespoons butter, melted
salt and pepper

Cut veal liver and ham into cubes. Seed bell peppers and cut into chunks. Remove stems from mushrooms and set aside. Slice ¼ of the mushroom caps and set aside with the stems.

Using metal skewers, thread liver, ham, mushroom caps and bell peppers, alternately. Brush well with butter, place over hot coals and cook for 20−25 minutes, turning and basting with butter, until liver is tender.

Meanwhile, add 2 tablespoons of butter to a heavy based pan with mushroom stems and sliced caps and cook, stirring, over hot coals for 3−4 minutes. Fold in noodles, stir and heat, cover and draw to the side of the fire to keep warm.

Serve veal liver and ham kebabs over hot noodles and mushrooms.

AVOCADO, APPLE AND CRAB SALAD (RECIPE PAGE 17) ▶

Kebabs of Liver on Onions

Serves: 4
Cooking time: 15–20 minutes
Barbecue on skewers over medium hot coals

1½ lbs (750 g) calves liver
3 tablespoons oil
4 tablespoons ground cumin
½ lb (125 g) bacon
salt
3 tablespoons lemon juice
3 tablespoons butter
4 medium onions, sliced
salt and pepper
Continental Potato Salad — see recipe page 38

Soak liver in a bowl of water for 1 hour, remove and pat dry, skin and discard tubes and cut meat into cubes. Heat oil in a pan, add meat and cook, turning often, until lightly browned. Remove liver from pan and roll in cumin, then wrap each cube in a piece of bacon. Thread onto skewers, sprinkle with salt, pepper, lemon juice and more cumin. Place kebabs over medium hot coals and cook for 15–20 minutes, turning often, until bacon is crisp. Meanwhile, add butter to the pan juices and heat, add onion slices and sauté until golden. Serve kebabs over onions with potato salad.

8

BARBECUED FISH WITH HERBS (RECIPE PAGE 17) ▶

Vegetables with Vinaigrette Sauce

Serves: 4
Cooking time: 15 minutes

4 medium sized potatoes
½ lb (250 g) green beans, trimmed and cut
boiling salted water
¼ lb (125 g) thick bacon
1 medium white onion, chopped
chopped parsley

Vinaigrette Sauce:
1 small white onion, chopped
1 large sprig of parsley
1 teaspoon sugar
1 teaspoon salt
3 tablespoons sweet pickle relish
4 tablespoons white vinegar
½ cup (125 ml) olive or salad oil

Combine all ingredients for vinaigrette sauce in a blender and blend for 3–4 minutes until creamy, pour into a jar, cover and chill for 25–30 minutes. Makes about ¾ cup (185 ml).
In separate pans of boiling water cook potatoes and beans for 12–15 minutes. Drain potatoes, peel and slice thickly and set aside to cool. Drain beans

and set aside to cool. Meanwhile cut the bacon into small chunks and cook in a pan until crisp, lift out and drain on paper towels.
Heap the beans into the center of a salad bowl and arrange potato slices around the edge. Scatter the bacon pieces and chopped onion on top. Spread vinaigrette sauce over the vegetables, cover and chill for 20–25 minutes. Sprinkle with parsley and serve with barbecued beef, lamb or veal.

Mushroom Salad

Serves: 4

1 lb (500 g) large mushrooms
4 tablespoons lemon juice
3 tablespoons chopped parsley
½ cup Italian Dressing — see recipe page 91

Wash and dry the mushrooms and slice thinly into a wooden salad bowl. Sprinkle lemon juice over, cover and chill for at least 30 minutes, basting occasionally. Sprinkle mushrooms with parsley and pour over the dressing. Gently toss and serve.

▼

TOMATO AND MINT SALAD (RECIPE PAGE 17) ▶

Cucumber Salad with Yogurt Dressing

Serves: 4

2 cucumbers, thinly sliced
1 small green bell pepper, seeded and thinly
   sliced
1 small red bell pepper, seeded and thinly sliced
watercress
black olives

Yogurt Dressing:
1¼ cups (300 ml) natural yogurt
4 tablespoons lemon juice
1 clove garlic, crushed
salt and lemon pepper

To make dressing, combine all ingredients in a blender and whirl on medium speed until thoroughly mixed and smooth.
Arrange cucumbers and cress on serving plates, pour over yogurt dressing and decorate top with green and red bell peppers and black olives.

▼

Mock Ham

Serves: 8–10
Cooking time: 2½–2¾ hour

4 lbs (2 kg) corned beef or corned leg of lamb
8 whole cloves
1 tablespoon brown sugar
1 tablespoon malt vinegar
1 small onion, halved
bouquet garni of thyme, parsley, and bay leaf

Rinse the leg in cold water and place in a large pan, cover with tepid water and bring to the boil. Pour off water and refill to cover lamb with tepid water. Add cloves, brown sugar, vinegar, onion halves and bouquet garni and bring to the boil. Reduce heat, cover and simmer gently for 2½–2¾ hours, until meat is tender. Remove pan from heat and allow the lamb to become cold. Lift out leg, drain well, then wrap in plastic film and refrigerate. Serve sliced thinly with a salad.

BARBECUED BEEF AND VEGETABLE BURGERS (RECIPE PAGE 20) ▶

Stuffed Tomatoes

Serves: 4

4 large tomatoes
salt and pepper
2 large apples
1 small carrot, diced
2 stalks celery, chopped finely
¼ cup (65 ml) lemon juice
3 tablespoons French Dressing — see recipe
   page 92
3 tablespoons sour cream
1 teaspoon prepared horseradish
pinch of tarragon
4 black olives

Cut a slice off the stem end of each tomato and scoop out the flesh, chop flesh and place in a bowl. Peel, core and dice the apples. Add apples, carrot and celery to tomato flesh, but reserve 4 pieces of each for garnish. Combine lemon juice, salt, French dressing, sour cream, horseradish and tarragon in a blender and whirl 1–2 minutes. Add tomato flesh, apples, carrot and celery and blend until almost smooth. Sprinkle tomato shells with salt and pepper, then fill with the mixture. Thread pieces of apple, carrot and celery onto 4 toothpicks and lay on top of tomatoes with a black olive. Chill, then serve.

BARBECUED SARDINES WITH RATATOUILLE (RECIPE PAGE 25) ▶

Fish and Tomato Salad

Serves: 6–8

1½ lb (750 g) cod fillets, diced
4 tablespoons lemon juice
salt and pepper
3 large firm tomatoes, peeled and roughly
   chopped
1 small green bell pepper, seeded and sliced
1 tablespoon capers
½ cup (125 ml) French Dressing — see recipe
   page 92
fennel for garnish

Place the fish in a glass dish and sprinkle with
lemon juice, salt and pepper, cover and chill for
3½–4 hours, basting occasionally. Drain off the
liquid and discard. Add tomatoes, bell pepper and
capers to the fish. Spread with French dressing, stir
gently, then cover and refrigerate for 1 hour, stirring
occasionally. Garnish with fennel. Serve with stuffed eggplant, vegetable platter and crusty bread.

Stuffed Eggplant

Serves: 6–8
Cooking time: 20–25 minutes

5 egg plants
salt
6 tablespoons oil
6 tablespoons butter
2 large onions, finely chopped
3 large tomatoes, peeled and chopped
2 cloves garlic, crushed
1 teaspoon thyme
1 tablespoon tomato paste
salt and pepper
grated cheddar cheese
dry breadcrumbs
Fish and Tomato Salad — see recipe
   this page

Cut eggplants in half, lengthways, slit around the
edge and criss cross flesh of each half. Sprinkle
flesh liberally with salt and set aside for 25–30
minutes, then drain and pat dry. Heat oil in a pan,
add eggplant halves, flesh side down, and cook for

7–8 minutes, turning once or twice. Lift from the pan and scoop out flesh and chop, but reserve the shells.

Melt half the butter in a pan, add onions and sauté until soft, add tomatoes, garlic, flesh, thyme, tomato paste, salt and pepper and simmer 6–7 minutes. Spoon the mixture into the eggplant shells, sprinkle with cheese and breadcrumbs and dot with remaining butter. Grill for 5–6 minutes until browned. Remove eggplant to a casserole dish to cool, then cover and chill. Serve with Fish and Tomato Salad, vegetable platter of avocado, cucumber, scallions and radish together with crusty bread.
(Illustrated on opposite page.)

Barbecued Fish with Herbs

Serves: 4–6
Cooking time: 35–40 minutes
Barbecue on grid over medium coals

2–3 lbs (1–1½ kg) whole fish, cleaned
6 tablespoons oil
2 teaspoons mixed herbs
salt and pepper
sprigs of sage
12 fresh prawns or shrimp
lemon wedges
Leek and Tomato Salad — see recipe page 54
Garlic Bread — see recipe page 85

Combine the oil and half the mixed herbs in a glass jar, cover and shake vigorously for 1–2 minutes, then let stand 15–20 minutes for oil to absorb the full flavor of the herbs.

Trim and wash fish and pat dry. Brush cavity of the fish with herb oil and sprinkle with remaining mixed herbs. Brush fish generously with herb oil and sprinkle with salt and pepper. Place fish on a greased barbecue grid over medium coals with sprigs of sage and cook for 35–40 minutes, until lightly browned on both sides, turn 2 or 3 times during cooking. Meanwhile, add prawns and cook for 10–12 minutes, turning once. Garnish with lemon wedges and serve with leek and tomato salad, and garlic breed.
(Illustrated on page 9.)

Tomato and Mint Salad

Serves: 4

4 medium, firm tomatoes, chilled
2 teaspoons sugar
salt and pepper
3 tablespoons lemon juice
6 tablespoons olive or salad oil
1 tablespoon chopped fresh mint
fresh mint leaves for garnish

Slice the tomatoes and place in a salad bowl, sprinkle with sugar, salt and pepper. Combine lemon juice, oil, salt, pepper and chopped mint in a jar, cover and shake vigorously, then pour over the tomatoes. Garnish with mint leaves. A good accompaniment for barbecued sirloin steak or lamb chops.
(Illustrated on page 11.)

Avocado, Apple and Crab Salad

Serves: 4–6

3 avocados, chilled
1 large apple, chilled
16 oz (440 g) can crabmeat, chilled
4 large crisp lettuce leaves
2–3 crisp celery tops
salt and pepper
½ cup (125 ml) Thousand Island Dressing —
see recipe page 89

Peel avocados, cut in half, discard seeds and slice. Peel and slice apple. Drain the crab. Place lettuce leaves in a salad bowl, add sliced avocados, apples, crabmeat and celery leaves and sprinkle with salt and pepper. Pour dressing over the salad and serve with barbecued pork or steak.
(Illustrated on page 7.)

Chicken on the Spit

Serves: 4
Cooking time: 1–1¼ hours
Barbecue on the spit over medium hot coals

2 small plump chickens or Cornish Hens
3 teaspoons salt
pepper
6 tablespoons butter, melted
Crunchy Coleslaw — see recipe page 39

Wash chickens and pat dry, sprinkle cavity with salt and pepper. Truss chickens and thread, firmly, on a spit rod, place on the spit over medium hot coals and cook for 40 minutes. Brush well with butter on all sides and cook a further 20–30 minutes, until tender, basting with butter frequently. Cut chickens in half and serve with coleslaw and hot French bread. Wash down with chilled white wine.

Piquant Rice Salad

Serves: 4
Cooking time: 15 minutes

1 cup of long grain rice
2 cups boiling salted water
1 medium green bell pepper, seeded and
    chopped
3 tablespoons golden raisins
3 tablespoons chopped scallions
1 tablespoon chopped parsley
salt and seasoned pepper
½ cup (125 ml) Italian Dressing — see recipe
    page 91

Cook rice in a pan of boiling salted water for 15 minutes, drain well, cool and place in a salad bowl. Add bell pepper, raisins, scallions, parsley, salt, pepper and dressing. Toss well and chill for 30 minutes. Serve with barbecued lamb or chicken.

Ragout of Artichokes

Serves: 6—8
Cooking time: 45—50 minutes
Cook in a casserole over low coals

12 artichokes
boiling salted water
4 tablespoons oil
2 large onions, chopped
3 large tomatoes, chopped
salt and seasoned pepper
2 cups (500 ml) dry white wine
1 tablespoon lemon juice
chopped parsley

Trim stems and outer leaves from artichokes. Plunge the heads into a pan of boiling salted water, cover and simmer for 30—35 minutes, until leaves can be gently pulled out. Drain well and arrange in a shallow flameproof casserole.

Meanwhile, heat oil in a pan, add onions and tomatoes and cook, stirring, for 6—7 minutes. Stir in salt, seasoned pepper, wine and lemon juice and bring to the boil, then pour mixture slowly over the artichokes to moisten all leaves. Cover and place at the side of barbecue to simmer for 12—15 minutes. Serve with barbecued meat or as a first course, with crusty bread.

Vegetable Platter in French Dressing

Serves: 4
Cooking time: 15 minutes

 4 medium potatoes, peeled and halved
 salted water
 ¼ lb (125 g) green beans, trimmed
 4 medium carrots
 2 medium cucumbers
 ½ cup (125 ml) French Dressing — see recipe
   page 92

In separate pans cook the potatoes and carrots in salted water for 15 minutes, drain and cool. Drop beans into a pan of boiling salted water, cover and cook for 6–8 minutes, drain and cool. Cut the cucumbers into quarters and place in a shallow dish with potatoes, carrots and beans. Spread the dressing over, baste well, cover and chill for 2–3 hours.
(Illustrated on page 13.)

Poached Fish with Hollandaise Sauce

Serves: 4–6
Cooking time: 40–45 minutes

 1½ lbs (750 g) fish fillets
 2 cups (500 ml) water
 1 small onion, stuck with 3 cloves
 4 peppercorns
 1 bay leaf
 top leaves of 1 celery stalk
 1 slice of lemon
 1 teaspoon salt

Quick Hollandaise Sauce:
 3 egg yolks
 2 tablespoons lemon juice
 1 tablespoon hot water
 ¾ cup (185 g) butter, melted
 1 teaspoon prepared mustard
 ½ teaspoon salt

Place water in a pan and add onion stuck with cloves, peppercorns, bay leaf, celery leaves, lemon slice and salt, bring to the boil, cover and simmer for 30 minutes. Strain liquid into another pan for Court-bouillon. Heat Court-bouillon to boiling, add fish, reduce heat, cover and simmer gently for 10–12 minutes. Drain fish and cool, then place in a salad bowl and chill.
Meanwhile, in a blender, combine egg yolks and lemon juice and blend 1–2 minutes, add hot water, then, on high speed, pour in butter through hole in lid insert, in a steady stream. Blend for 2 minutes, add mustard and salt and blend 1 minutes. Turn sauce into a bowl and chill. Serve fish and sauce in separate dishes.
(Illustrated on page 5.)

Barbecued Beef and Vegetable Burgers

Serves: 4
Cooking time: 18–20 minutes
Barbecue on grid over hot coals

 1 lb (500 g) ground beef
 2 medium carrots, grated
 1 stalk of celery, finely chopped
 ½ teaspoon thyme
 ½ teaspoon rosemary
 salt and pepper
 4 hamburger buns
 1 tablespoon butter, melted
 sprigs of rosemary for garnish
 prepared mustard
 pickled sweet and sour gherkins

In a bowl combine meat with carrots, celery, thyme, rosemary, salt and pepper and mix thoroughly. Shape into 8 patties and refrigerate for 30–40 minutes. Place burgers on the grid over hot coals and cook for 18–20 minutes, turning once.
Meanwhile, cut buns in half and place on the grid over hot coals to toast on each side after brushing with butter. Serve beef and vegetable burgers on hot buns with mustard and pickled sweet and sour gherkins.
(Illustrated on page 13.)

Patio Picnic

Serves: 4–6

26 oz (820 g) can beets, drained
4 medium tomatoes
6 hard boiled eggs
6–8 pickled cucumbers
Vegetable Platter in French Dressing — see
   recipe page 20
Poached Fish with Hollandaise Sauce — see
   recipe page 20
crunchy French bread

Chop the beets into bite size pieces and place in a bowl. Cut the tomatoes into quarters and place 4 quarters around beets. Shell and halve the eggs and place in a separate bowl with remaining tomato quarters. Halve the pickled cucumbers and place in another bowl. Serve with chilled Vegetable Platter in French Dressing, Poached Fish with Hollandaise Sauce, and crunchy bread.
(Illustrated on page 5.)

Barbecued Steak, Chops and Sausages

Serves: 4
Cooking time: 1 hour
Barbecue on the grid over medium hot coals

2 large barbecue steaks
4 lamb or pork chops
1 lb (500 g) thick sausages
4 Foil Wrapped Potatoes — see recipe page 43

Barbecue Sauce:
1 tablespoon oil
1 small onion, finely chopped
1 clove garlic, crushed
2 teaspoons prepared mustard
2 tablespoons tomato catsup
1 teaspoon Worcestershire sauce
dash of Tabasco sauce
salt and pepper
½ cup (125 ml) flat beer

Prepare and start cooking potatoes. Place sausages in a pan, cover with cold water and bring to the boil, simmer 2–3 minutes and drain well.
To make the sauce, heat oil in a pan, add onion and garlic and sauté until onion is soft. Stir in mustard, tomato, Worcestershire and Tabasco sauces, salt, pepper and beer. Bring to the boil and simmer 2–3 minutes, then set aside.
Brush the steaks, chops and sausages on all sides with sauce and place on the grid over medium hot coals. Cook for 15–18 minutes, turning often and basting with the sauce.
Cut the steaks in half and serve with chops and sausages, potatoes, lettuce salad and crusty French bread.
(Illustrated on front cover & page 4.)

Barbecued Mixed Grill

Serves: 6
Cooking time: 18–20 minutes
Barbecue on the grid over medium hot coals

6 thick pork sausages, par-boiled
2 veal kidneys, trimmed and thickly sliced
6 slices of trimmed calves liver
6 strips of lean bacon
4 tablespoons oil
3 tablespoons milk
6 medium tomatoes, halved
3 bananas, peeled and split in half
2 apples, cored and thickly sliced

Place par-boiled sausages, kidney and liver slices and bacon in a shallow bowl and add the oil. Baste and set aside for 2½–3 hours, turning and basting the meats occasionally. Lift out sausages and dip into the milk, then place on the grid over medium hot coals and cook for 18–20 minutes, turning often. Add kidney slices to grid and cook 12–15 minutes, turning often, then add liver slices and bacon and cook for 10–12 minutes, turning often. Place tomato halves, banana and apple slices at the side of the grid and cook until golden brown on each side. Serve food hot with catsup and prepared mustard on the side. Great with rye bread and chilled beer.

Mackerel with Spiced Mustard Sauce

Serves: 4–6
Cooking time: 18–20 minutes
Barbecue in wire grid over medium hot coals

    4–6 mackerel, cleaned
    3 tablespoons French mustard
    1 tablespoon flour
    ¼ teaspoon cayenne pepper
    1 teaspoon seasoned pepper
    salt
    lemon wedges
    Goddess Salad — see recipe page 54

Combine mustard, flour, cayenne and seasoned pepper and mix well for spiced mustard sauce. Wash fish and pat dry. Spread evenly all over with the sauce and sprinkle with salt. Place fish in a hinged wire grid and cook over medium hot coals for 18–20 minutes, turning and basting often with the sauce. Serve fish with lemon wedges, salad and hot French bread.

Special Cucumber Salad

Serves: 4

    2 green cucumbers
    2 teaspoons salt

Dressing:
4 tablespoons salad oil
1 tablespoon white vinegar
1 teaspoon French mustard
6 tablespoons natural yogurt
dash of pepper
2 tablespoons chopped parsley

Peel and thinly slice the cucumber and place in a glass dish, sprinkle with salt and set aside for 1 hour. Wash cucumber slices thoroughly with cold water, squeeze out as much liquid as possible, then arrange in a salad bowl. Combine in a bowl the oil, vinegar, mustard, yogurt and pepper and mix very well for a dressing, then pour over cucumbers, sprinkle with parsley and toss.

BARBECUED MACKEREL WITH FRIED APPLE RINGS (RECIPE PAGE 24) ▶

Barbecued Mackerel with Fried Apple Rings

Serves: 4–6
Cooking time: 18–20 minutes
Barbecue on grid over medium hot coals

6 mackerel, cleaned
1 tablespoon oil
salt and pepper
4 large cooking apples
6 tablespoons butter

Wash fish and pat dry, brush with oil and sprinkle with salt and pepper. Place fish on the barbecue grid over medium hot coals and cook 8–10 minutes on each side. Meanwhile, peel and core apples and slice into thick rings. Melt butter in a heavy pan beside the fish, add apple slices, a few at a time, and cook until golden brown on both sides. Serve mackerel and apple rings with a tossed salad.
(Illustrated on page 23.)

Scallop Kebabs with White Butter Sauce

Serves: 4
Cooking time: 10–12 minutes
Barbecue on skewers over medium hot coals

1½ lbs (750 g) scallops
24 bay leaves
4 tablespoons butter, melted
salt and pepper
boiled rice

White Butter Sauce:
Cooking time: 20–25 minutes
3 scallions, chopped
½ cup (125 ml) wine vinegar
bouquet garni of thyme, parsley and bay leaf
salt and pepper
pinch of cayenne pepper
6 tablespoons butter, softened
3 tablespoons cream, whipped

To make white butter sauce: In a pan combine scallions, wine vinegar, bouquet garni, salt and pepper, bring to the boil and cook until liquid is reduced by half (approximately ¼ cup). Strain liquid into the top of a double boiler and cool. Place top of double boiler over barely simmering water, add egg yolks and cayenne pepper and whisk the mixture well, then gradually add the butter, a little at a time, whisking constantly, until the sauce starts to thicken. Fold in whipped cream, then pour sauce into a bowl and allow to cool.
Wash and dry the scallops and thread, alternately, with bay leaves on skewers, brush with melted butter and sprinkle with salt and pepper. Place kebabs over medium hot coals and cook for 10–12 minutes, turning frequently and basting with butter. Serve with white butter sauce and boiled rice, garnish with lemon wedges, parsley and prawns (optional).
(Illustrated on page 1.)

Kebabs of Veal, Onion and Pineapple

Serves: 4–6
Cooking time: 20–25 minutes
Barbecue on skewers over hot coals

¾ lb (375 g) lean veal, thinly sliced
2 medium onions, cut in wedges
16 oz (450 g) can sliced pineapple, drained
1 tablespoon honey
2 tablespoons pineapple syrup
2 tablespoons lemon juice
1 tablespoon butter

Combine honey, pineapple syrup, lemon juice and butter in a pan and heat, stirring, until bubbly, for a baste. Cut veal slices into 1″ (2½ cm) wide stirps. Cut pineapple into pieces. Thread veal, onions and pineapple, alternately, on skewers and brush with the baste. Cook over hot coals for 18–20 minutes, until meat is teander, turning and brushing often with the baste.

Barbecued Sardines with Ratatouille

Serves: 4
Cooking time: 10–12 minutes
Barbecue in wire basket over medium coals

1½ lbs (750 g) sardines, cleaned
lemon juice
3 tablespoons butter, melted
Ratatouille — see recipe page 35
Old Fashioned Damper — see recipe page 85

Place sardines in a wire basket and cook over medium coals for 10–12 minutes, turning basket 2 or 3 times. Brush fish with lemon juice and melted butter. Serve with ratatouille and hot crusty bread. *(Illustrated on page 15.)*

Barbecued Cheese Stuffed Steak

Serves: 4
Cooking time: 15–18 minutes
Barbecue on the grid over medium hot coals

2 lbs (1 kg) rump steak (2 slices)
2 oz (60 g) blue cheese
2 tablespoons chopped parsley
2 teaspoons finely chopped chives
6 tablespoons butter, softened
salt and pepper
Coleslaw Special — see recipe page 72
Garlic Bread — see recipe page 85

Slit a pocket in each slice of steak. Mix cheese, parsley, chives and 3 tablespoons butter together until smooth, spoon into the pocket of each steak and fasten with skewers. Sprinkle steaks with salt and pepper on each side, place on the grid over medium hot coals and cook for 15–18 minutes, turning often. Brush meat with remaining butter while cooking. Cut steaks in half and serve with coleslaw and hot garlic bread.

Barbecued Snapper

Serves: 4
Cooking time: 25–30 minutes
Barbecue in foil over hot coals

3 lbs (1½ kg) whole snapper, cleaned
2 teaspoons salt
3 tablespoons lemon juice
1 lemon, cut in slices
1 small onion, sliced
3 tablespoons butter
sprinkle of pepper
1 tablespoon chopped parsley

Pat fish dry and sprinkle inside and out with salt and lemon juice. Make 2–3 slashes in the skin on each side and cover slashes with lemon and onion slices. Place fish on doubled aluminium foil, dull side out, and dot with butter. Sprinkle with pepper and parsley and wrap securely. Place on the grid over hot coals and cook for 25–30 minutes, until tender, turning 2–3 times.

Barbecued Corn in Foil

Serves: 4–6
Cooking time: 18–20 minutes
Barbecue on the grid over hot coals

4–6 ears of corn, husked
6 tablespoons butter, melted
salt and pepper
3 tablespoons milk
¼ teaspoon sugar

Place each corn cob on double aluminium foil, dull side out, brush with butter and sprinkle with salt and pepper, wrap corn, leaving one end open. Mix milk and sugar together and add through open end, then close. Place on the grid over hot coals and cook for 18–20 minutes, turning often, until tender. Serve hot with extra butter, salt and pepper.

▲ VEAL, BACON AND MUSHROOM KEBABS (RECIPE PAGE 28)

▲ BAKED APPLES (RECIPE PAGE 28)

Festive Picnic Spread

Serves: 4–6

¼ lb (125 g) sliced salami
1 paprika sausage, sliced
½ lb (250 g) sliced leg ham
¼ lb (125 g) sliced ham sausage
6 oz can pâté de foie gras
6 oz can sliced beets, drained
14 oz can pickled red cabbage, drained
14 oz can hearts of palm, drained
4 oz can pickled herrings in onion sauce
7 oz can salmon, drained, with lemon
    slices
10–12 gherkins, with lemon ring and parsley
black and green olives

1 lb (500 g) cooked prawns, washed
fluffy white rice mixed with walnuts
Saffron Rice Salad mixed with raisins — see
    recipe page 85
4 tomatoes, washed
3 spring onions, washed and trimmed
1 bunch of fennel, washed
bunch small radishes, washed
White Salad Cream — see recipe page 89

Place each ingredient in individual covered plastic dishes and chill overnight. At the picnic spot, open plastic dishes and arrange. Sprinkle salad cream with chopped chives. Serve food with crusty French bread and wash down with dry white wine.

Baked Apples

Serves: 4
Cooking time: 40–45 minutes
Barbecue in cocotte over medium hot coals

4 large red apples
2 tablespoons butter
4 tablespoons red currant jam
4 tablespoons sugar
½ cup (125 ml) water
whipped cream

Core each apple well to make a hole through, and fill each hole with 2 teaspoons of butter and 2 teaspoons jam. Place apples in an earthenware casserole. Mix sugar, water and remaining jam together and spoon around the apple. Cover and cook on the grid over medium hot coals for 40–45 minutes, until tender. Serve apples with juices poured over them and topped with whipped cream.
(Illustrated on page 26.)

Veal, Bacon and Mushroom Kebabs

Serves: 4
Cooking time: 20–25 minutes
Barbecue on skewers over hot coals

1 lb (500 g) lean veal
½ lb (250 g) thick piece of bacon
¼ lb (125 g) medium size mushrooms, stemmed
4 tomatoes, sliced thickly

Marinade:
½ cup (125 ml) oil
juice of 1 small lemon
1 tablespoon tomato catsup
1 teaspoon thyme
½ teaspoon basil
½ teaspoon ground bay leaves
salt and pepper

To make marinade: In a bowl combine oil, lemon juice, catsup, thyme, basil, ground bay leaves, salt and pepper and mix well. Add veal and bacon to the bowl and baste with the marinade, then set bowl aside for 2½–3 hours, basting occasionally. Drain veal and bacon well and reserve marinade. Thread veal, bacon and mushroom caps, alternately, on metal skewers and place over hot coals to cook for 20–25 minutes, until veal is tender, turning frequently and basting with reserved marinade. Meanwhile, place tomato slices on oiled hot plate and cook 2–3 minutes each side.
(Illustrated on page 26.)

King Prawn Kebabs

Serves: 4
Cooking time: 10–12 minutes
Barbecue on skewers over medium coals

1½ lbs (750 g) king prawns
fresh tarragon for garnish (optional)
Greek Salad — see recipe page 50
Garlic Bread — see recipe page 85

Marinade:
½ cup (125 ml) oil
3 tablespoons lemon juice
1 clove garlic, crushed
1 tablespoon tarragon vinegar
salt and pepper

To make marinade: Combine, in a jar, oil, lemon juice, garlic, tarragon vinegar, salt and pepper, cover and shake vigorously to mix. Place prawns on a dish and add the marinade. Cover and set aside in a cool place, to marinate, for 4–5 hours, basting occasionally. Lift out prawns and thread onto metal skewers. Cook over medium coals for 10–12 minutes, turning 2–3 times and brushing with marinade. Serve prawns hot, garnished with fresh tarragon leaves, with salad and hot garlic bread.
(Illustrated on page 31.)

Baked Potatoes

Serves: 4—6
Cooking time: 1 hour
Barbecue in foil on the grid or in hot ashes

4—6 large even-sized potatoes
4 tablespoons oil
salt and pepper
3 strips of bacon, cooked and crumbled
6 tablespoons sour cream
chopped chives

Scrub potatoes, dry and prick each one 4—5 times with a skewer. Brush with oil and sprinkle with salt and pepper. Wrap each potato in aluminium foil to seal. Cook over hot coals on the grid, or in the coals for 1 hour, turning occasionally, until potatoes are soft. Cut a cross on the top of each potato and squeeze to open up. Serve with bacon, sour cream and chives.

Watercress and Mushroom Salad

1 bunch watercress
6 crisp lettuce leaves
¼ lb (125 g) button mushrooms
4 oz (100 g) whole walnut kernels
4 tablespoons salad oil
1 tablespoon white vinegar
1 clove garlic, crushed
salt and black pepper
1 tablespoon chopped parsley
1 tablespoon chopped chives

Wash, trim and pat dry watercress and lettuce leaves and tear into bite size pieces. Place in a salad bowl, cover and chill for 30 minutes. Wipe mushrooms, trim the stems and slice thinly into a bowl and add walnut kernels. Combine oil in a jar with vinegar, garlic, salt and black pepper, cover and shake well, until mixture thickens slightly. Pour over mushrooms and walnuts and mix lightly, then add to watercress and lettuce, sprinkle with parsley and chives, toss and serve.

Barbecued Lamb Breasts

Serves: 4
Cooking time: 1½—1¾ hours
Barbecue on the spit over medium hot coals

4 lamb breasts, boned and trimmed
Honey and Wine Marinade for Lamb — see recipe page 87
1½ cups cooked rice
2 slices bacon, minced
1 medium onion, minced
3 tablespoons white wine
1 teaspoon rosemary
1 tablespoon chopped parsley
salt and pepper

Place the lamb breasts in a glass or enamel dish, add marinade, baste and set aside for 1—1¼ hours to marinate, basting occasionally. Drain meat, pat dry and place flat, skin side down, on a flat surface; reserve the marinade.
Combine rice, bacon, onion, wine, rosemary, parsley, salt and pepper in a bowl and mix well. Divide mixture in half on to each lamb breast for stuffing. Roll lamb firmly and tie with string. Thread spit rod through the center of each rolled breast and secure. Cook on the spit over medium hot coals for 1½—1¾ hours, until tender. Baste with reserved marinade in last 30—40 minutes of cooking.

Barbecued Bananas

Serves: 4—6
Cooking time: 12—15 minutes
Barbecue on grid over medium coals

6 large bananas

Do not peel bananas but place on the grid, in their skins, over medium coals and cook for 12—15 minutes. Remove bananas from the heat, slice in half lengthways and serve. An added flavor for barbecued chicken.

Barbecued Sausages on Onions

Serves: 4
Cooking time: 15–18 minutes
Barbecue on grid over medium coals

   8 paprika pork sausages
   3 large onions
   4 tablespoons oil
   ¼ teaspoon ground cloves
   ¼ teaspoon thyme
   salt
   4 bread rolls
   3 tablespoons butter, melted
   prepared mustard

Peel and slice onions. Heat half the oil in a heavy pan over coals, add onions, cloves, thyme and salt and sauté until onions are soft, draw to the side of barbecue, cover and keep warm.
Meanwhile, brush sausages with remaining oil, place on a grid and cook over medium coals, turning often, for 15–18 minutes.
Split bread rolls and brush with butter, spoon onions on lower half, add 1 or 2 sausages and close roll. Serve with mustard.

Red Bell Peppers in Garlic Oil

Serves: 4
Cooking time: 10–12 minutes
Barbecue on the grid over hot coals

   4 red bell peppers
   ½ cup (125 ml) oil
   2 cloves garlic, crushed
   1 small onion, minced

Wash and dry bell peppers and place on the grid over hot coals and cook for 10–12 minutes, turning frequently. Remove from heat, cool, cut in half, seed, then cut lengthways into thick slices. Place in a flameproof casserole with oil, garlic and onion and let stand 25–30 minutes to marinate, stirring occasionally. Place casserole on the side of barbecue to heat through while cooking steak or chops. Bell peppers can also be cooked in a moderate oven for 10–12 minutes, then marinated and chilled.

▼

KING PRAWN KEBABS (RECIPE PAGE 28) ▶

Chilled Ratatouille

Serves: 4–6
Cooking time: 40–45 minutes

  2 tablespoons oil
  1 clove garlic, crushed
  1 medium eggplant, peeled and diced
  1 small green bell pepper, seeded and sliced
  1 large tomato, peeled and chopped
  1 large onion, chopped
  3–4 small zucchini, sliced
  salt and pepper

Heat oil in a heatproof casserole dish, add garlic and cook 1 minute, add eggplant, bell pepper, onion, tomato and zucchini in layers; season each layer with salt and pepper. Add a few more drops of oil to the surface, cover and simmer gently for 30 minutes, gently moving the vegetables occasionally. Uncover and simmer a further 10–15 minutes to reduce liquid a little. Remove dish from heat and allow to cool, then refrigerate, covered, for at least 2 hours and serve.
(Illustrated on opposite page.)

Savoury Meat Loaf

Serves: 6–8
Cooking time: 1 hour
Oven: 180°C   350°F

  1 lb (500 g) ground lean beef
  1 lb (500 g) ground lean pork
  1½ cups soft breadcrumbs
  ¼ cup white wine or water
  1 medium onion, finely chopped
  2 tablespoons tomato catsup
  2 teaspoons Worcestershire Sauce
  dash of Tabasco sauce
  1 teaspoon dry mustard
  1 tablespoon chopped parsley
  ½ teaspoon chopped chives
  1½ teaspoons salt
  seasoned pepper
  2 eggs
  Endive, Cheese and Tomato Salad — see
    recipe this page
  Blender Mayonnaise — see recipe page 92
  Chilled Ratatouille — see recipe this page

Soak breadcrumbs in a bowl with wine or water until all liquid is absorbed. Combine all other ingredients on a large dish, add moist crumbs and mix well, using hands. Turn mixture into a greased loaf pan and pack down, cover and chill for 1 hour. Cook in a pre-heated moderate oven for 1 hour. Remove from oven and cool, then turn out loaf, wrap and refrigerate. Place meat loaf on a bed of curly endive or shredded lettuce leaves and slice. Serve with salad, mayonnaise, chilled ratatouille and crunchy French bread.
(Illustrated on opposite page.)

Endive, Cheese and Tomato Salad

Serves: 4

  1 bunch curly endive
  ¼ lb (125 g) Gruyère cheese
  2 medium tomatoes, chilled
  ½ cup (125 ml) Blender Mayonnaise — see
    recipe page 92

Wash, dry and crisp the endive and break into bite size pieces. Cut the cheese into small cubes and slice the tomatoes into wedges. Place endive, cheese and tomatoes in a salad bowl and toss, then add the mayonnaise and serve.
(Illustrated on opposite page.)

Carrot and Pineapple Salad

Serves: 6–8

  1 lb (500 g) young carrots
  1 medium size pineapple
  ½ cup (125 ml) orange juice
  1 tablespoon chopped mint

Grate the carrots and place in a salad bowl. Peel the pineapple, core and slice, then cut into small cubes and add to the carrots. Sprinkle orange juice over and toss well, then chill for at least 2 hours. Add mint and toss again at serving.

Veal and Eggplant Kebabs

Serves: 4
Cooking time: 18–20 minutes
Barbecue on skewers over hot coals

1½ lbs (750 g) veal
Soy and Ginger Marinade — see recipe page 88
1 small eggplant
salt and pepper
2 teaspoons lemon juice
3 medium onions, quartered

Cut the veal into 1" (2½ cm) cubes and place in a bowl, add the marinade and baste. Refrigerate for 2½–3 hours, basting occasionally. Peel the eggplant and dice, place in a bowl and sprinkle with salt. Set bowl aside for 30 minutes, then drain eggplant, rinse under cold water and pat dry. Sprinkle with pepper and lemon juice. Lift out veal and drain.

Thread veal, eggplant and onion quarters, alternately, on skewers, and brush kebabs with the marinade. Place over hot coals and cook for 18–20 minutes, until meat is tender, turning often and basting with the marinade.

Barbecued Glazed Pineapple Rings

Serves: 6–8
Cooking time: 8–10 minutes
Barbecue on the grid over medium coals

1 medium pineapple
6 tablespoons honey
3 tablespoons prepared mustard

Core and trim the pineapple and cut into rings. Mix the honey and mustard in a pan and warm, then brush over the pineapple rings and place on the grid over medium coals. Cook for 8–10 minutes, turning and basting with the glaze, uuntil lightly browned. Serve hot with barbecued pork or steak.

Artichoke Hearts with Vinaigrette

Serves: 4

12 oz (400 g) can of artichoke hearts
4 tablespoons salad oil
2 tablespoons white vinegar
clove garlic, crushed
salt and pepper
chopped parsley

To prepare vinaigrette, combine oil, vinegar, garlic, salt and pepper in a jar, cover and shake vigorously until creamy and smooth. Chill for 1 hour.
Drain artichoke hearts well and arrange in a shallow serving dish. Sprinkle with vinaigrette and sprinkle with parsley.

Barbecued Pork Chops with Spicy Sauce

Serves: 6
Cooking time: 25–30 minutes
Barbecue on the grid over medium coals

6 pork loin chops, 1" (2½ cm) thick
3 tablespoons butter, melted
salt and pepper

Spicy Sauce:
4 tablespoons malt vinegar
½ cup (125 ml) tomato catsup
3 teaspoons sugar
½ teaspoon ground cloves
½ teaspoon prepared mustard
½ teaspoon ground bay leaves
salt and pepper

To make the sauce, combine vinegar, tomato sauce, sugar, cloves, mustard, ground bay leaves, salt and pepper in a heavy pan and place on the barbecue over low heat to simmer gently for 25–30 minutes.
Meanwhile, brush pork chops with butter and sprinkle with salt and pepper and set aside for

8–10 minutes, then place chops on the grid over medium coals and cook for 8 minutes, turn and brush with the spicy sauce, cook a further 8 minutes, turn and baste. Turn chops once or twice more, basting each time and serve hot, with remaining spicy sauce on the side. Delicious with cucumber salad, fluffy white rice and hot garlic bread.

Barbecued Ham and Pineapple

Serves: 4
Cooking time: 6–7 minutes
Barbecue on the grid over hot coals

4 thick ham steaks
8 canned pineapple rings, drained
½ teaspoon dry mustard
½ teaspoon ground cloves
salt and pepper
3 tablespoons lemon juice
1 teaspoon soy sauce
4 tablespoons honey

Mix mustard, cloves, salt, pepper and lemon juice in a bowl until smooth, stir in soy sauce and honey until blended, for a baste. Brush ham steaks and pineapple rings with the baste and place on the grid over hot coals. Cook for 6–7 minutes, turning often and brushing with the baste.

Ratatouille

Serves: 4–6
Cooking time: 45–50 minutes
Barbecue in a casserole over low heat coals

⅓ cup (85 ml) olive or salad oil
1 clove garlic, sliced thinly
2 large onions, thinly sliced
2 large green bell peppers, seeded and chopped
1 medium eggplant, peeled and sliced
1 extra clove garlic, crushed
½ lb (250 g) zucchini, sliced
4 large tomatoes, peeled and sliced
salt and pepper

Heat half the oil in a flameproof casserole with the sliced garlic. Add in layers the onions, bell peppers, eggplant, extra garlic, zucchini and tomatoes. Sprinkle each layer with salt and pepper and pour the remainder of the oil over the top. Cover and heat, then transfer to the barbecue over low heat and cook for 40–45 minutes to sweat the vegetables and bring out all the flavors. Move casserole over medium hot coals, remove lid and cook for 5 minutes to thicken the sauce. Serve hot with barbecued meats and fish.

Turkey on the Spit

Serves: 8–10
Cooking time: 3–3¼ hour
Barbecue on the spit over medium coals

10 lb (5 kg) plump turkey, dressed
3 cups (750 ml) chicken cube stock
½ cup (125 g) butter, melted

Stuffing:
1 lb (500 g) pork, ground
1 medium onion, minced
¼ lb (125 g) bacon, minced
2 teaspoons mixed herbs
1 cup soft breadcrumbs
1 egg beaten
white wine

Combine pork, onion, bacon, herbs, breadcrumbs and egg in a bowl, moisten with wine and mix for stuffing.
Place turkey in a large pan with chicken stock and bring to the boil, reduce heat, cover and simmer for 30 minutes. Lift out turkey, drain and cool to handle. Fill cavity with stuffing and close with a skewer, tie bird with stiring and thread the spit rod through the center, neck to tail, and secure. Brush turkey well with melted butter and place on the spit over medium coals. Place foil tray beneath bird to catch drippings and prevent flames flaring. Cook for 2½–2¾ hour, until tender, basting often with butter. Lift turkey from the spit onto a carving tray, remove rod and allow bird to rest for 5 minutes. Carve and serve.

▲ COOKED CUCUMBER AND CARROT SALAD (RECIPE PAGE 38)

▲ CHARCOAL COOKED MUSSELS (RECIPE PAGE 38)

Bacon and Egg Salad

Serves: 4

½ lb (250 g) Canadian bacon
3 eggs
2 scallions
6–7 crisp lettuce leaves
salt and seasoned pepper
½ cup (125 ml) Vinaigrette Dressing — see
recipe page 91

Cut bacon into pieces and cook in a pan until crisp, remove from pan, drain on paper towels and chill. Prick round end of each egg with a darning needle or thumb tack and place in a pan, cover with cold water, bring to the boil and cook for 10 minutes. Drain eggs and run under cold water to cool quickly, then peel, cut into wedges and chill. Chop the scallions finely.

Arrange lettuce leaves in a salad bowl, add bacon, egg wedges and scallions, sprinkle with salt and seasoned pepper. Pour vinaigrette dressing over and serve immediately. A good accompaniment to barbecued pork chops, lamb chops or sausages.

Barbecued Steak Diane

Serves: 4
Cooking time: 6–8 minutes
Barbecue on the grid over medium hot coals

4 thick fillet steaks
4 tablespoons butter
2 cloves garlic, crushed
3 tablespoons lemon juice
1 tablespoon Worcestershire sauce
salt and pepper
Fennel and Lemon Salad — see recipe page 85
Continental Potato Salad — see recipe page 38
Garlic Bread — see recipe page 85

Flatten steaks with a mallet. In a pan melt butter, add garlic and sauté for 2 minutes. Brush steaks with garlic butter and barbecue for 3–4 minutes on each side, for rare, basting frequently with garlic butter. Combine lemon juice, Worcestershire sauce, salt and pepper with remaining garlic butter. Heat and pour over steaks. Serve with salads and bread.

Cooked Cucumber and Carrot Salad

Serves: 4–6
Cooking time: 25–30 minutes

2 cucumbers, sliced in chunks
2 large carrots, sliced
1 medium onion, chopped finely
1 clove garlic, crushed
bouquet garni of thyme, parsley and bay leaf
6 tablespoons oil
juice of 1 lemon
2 cups (500 ml) white wine
salt and pepper
½ teaspoon coriander

Place cucumbers, carrots, onion, garlic and bouquet garni in a pan. Combine oil, lemon juice, wine, salt, pepper and coriander in a glass jar, cover and shake vigorously to mix, then pour over the vegetables. Cover pan and cook gently for 25–30 minutes. Cool, turn out into a bowl and chill. (Illustrated on page 36.)

Charcoal Cooked Mussels

Serves: 4
Cooking time: 10–12 minutes
Barbecue on hot plate over hot coals

4 lbs (2 kg) mussels in the shell
salt and pepper
lemon wedges
spring onions
French bread

Wash mussels thoroughly and spread on hot plate over hot coals. Cook for 10–12 minutes, until they open. Serve mussels as they open with salt, pepper, lemon wedges and crunchy French bread. Wash down with red wine.
(Illustrated on page 36.)

Tomato and Sour Cream Salad

Serves: 4–6

4 large firm ripe tomatoes
2 medium white onions
1 tablespoon sugar
3 teaspoons salt
8 oz (300 ml) carton light sour cream

Thinly slice tomatoes and onions and place, in layers, in a salad bowl, sprinkle sugar and salt between each layer, finishing with a layer of tomatoes. Spoon sour cream over the tomatoes, cover and chill for 2 hours. Do not toss before serving.

Continental Potato Salad

Serves: 6
Cooking time: 15–18 minutes

2 lbs (1 kg) new potatoes
salted water
1 medium white onion
1 Granny Smith apple
2 dill pickles
4 tablespoons salad oil
1 tablespoon white vinegar
salt and pepper
½ cup (125 ml) mayonnaise
1 tablespoon chopped parsley

In a pan of water, cook the potatoes in their jackets for 15–18 minutes, lift out potatoes and allow to cool a little, peel and chill for 2–3 hours. Dice potatoes and place in a salad bowl. Mince the onion; peel, core and dice the apple; chop the pickled cucumbers and add to the potatoes. Combine oil, vinegar, salt and pepper in a jar, cover and shake well to mix; add to the salad and toss gently. Spoon mayonnaise over the salad and toss again. Cover and chill for 2 hours, toss and serve sprinkled with parsley.

Chicken Satay with Peanut Sauce

Serves: 4–6
Cooking time: 8–10 minutes
Barbecue on bamboo sticks over hot coals

1½ lbs (750 g) diced chicken

Peanut Sauce:
3 tablespoons butter
1 small onion, minced
1 clove garlic, crushed
3 tablespoons peanut butter
3 teaspoons lemon juice
3 teaspoons soy sauce
⅓ cup (85 ml) cream

For peanut sauce, melt butter in a pan, add onion and garlic and sauté for 2–3 minutes. Stir in peanut butter, lemon juice and soy sauce until blended and heated. Remove pan from heat and cool. At serving, fold in cream until smooth and pour into a shallow dish.
Thread diced chicken pieces onto bamboo satay sticks and cook over hot coals for 3–4 minutes, until tender, turning frequently. Dip in peanut sauce and serve immediately. Beef, lamb or pork may be used in place of chicken.

Stuffed Dates and Bacon

Serves: 4–6
Cooking time: 10–12 minutes
Barbecue on skewers over medium hot coals

24 dates
¼ lb (125 g) cheddar cheese, cut into 24 pieces
½ lb (250 g) bacon, cut into 24 strips

Pit the dates and stuff each with a piece of cheese. Wrap each date in a strip of bacon and thread onto bamboo skewers. Cook over medium hot coals for 10–12 minutes, turning often, until bacon is crisp. Serve hot, as an appetiser.

Crunchy Coleslaw

Serves: 4–6

¼ head of cabbage
3 carrots
2 Granny Smith apples
2 stalks white celery
salt and pepper
6 tablespoons mayonnaise
6 tablespoons cream
½ cup chopped walnuts
1 tablespoon chopped parsley

Shred the cabbage finely; grate the carrots; peel, core and chop the apples; chop the celery and place all in a salad bowl, sprinkle with salt and pepper and toss. Combine mayonnaise and cream together and pour over the salad. Toss well, then cover and chill for at least 1 hour. At serving, sprinkle salad with walnuts and parsley and toss.

Toberua Kokonda

Serves: 8–10
Cooking time: 2–3 minutes

2 lbs (1 kg) firms, white fish
6 tablespoons lime or lemon juice
1 large white onion, finely chopped
2 scallions, finely chopped
1 small carrot, grated
½ small red chili, very finely chopped
¼ green bell pepper, finely chopped
salt and pepper
1½ cups shredded coconut
¾ cup (185 ml) milk

Skin, bone and dice the fish and place, with lime juice, in a glass bowl; stir and baste, then set aside for 1 hour to marinate, stirring occasionally with a wooden spoon, until fish is opaque. Drain fish very well and place in a glass bowl with onion, scallions, carrot, chili, bell pepper, salt and pepper. Combine coconut and milk in a pan and bring slowly to the boil, cool, then mix in a blender until smooth. Pour over the fish and stir, chill for 2 hours and serve in small bowls as an appetiser.

Cabbage Salad with Salami and Eggs

Serves: 4–6

 4 cups finely shredded cabbage
 3 tablespoons salad oil
 1 tablespoon vinegar
 ¼ teaspoon salt
 dash of seasoned pepper
 2 hard boiled eggs, cut in wedges
 4 slices of salami, cut in bite size pieces
 10–12 black olives
 4 tablespoons mayonnaise

Place cabbage in a plastic bowl. Combine oil, vinegar, salt and seasoned pepper in a jar, cover and shake vigorously to mix well, then pour over the cabbage. Cover and chill 3–4 hours, shaking bowl occasionally. Turn cabbage into a salad bowl and top with egg wedges, salami pieces, black olives and mayonnaise.

Eggs in Aspic

Serves: 4

 1 slice of ham, cut in 4 pieces
 1 small tomato, quartered
 4 sprigs of parsley
 4 poached eggs
 2 envelopes (20 g) gelatin
 ½ cup (125 ml) hot water
 3 cups (750 ml) beef cube stock
 ½ cup (125 ml) white wine
 4 lettuce leaves
 pickled onions
 stuffed green olives
 black olives

In each gelation mold place a piece of ham, a quarter of tomato, sprig of parsley and a poached egg. Sprinkle gelatin over 1 quart of hot water and stir briskly until dissolved, stir in stock and wine, mix well and cool. Pour gelatin into molds and refrigerate until set. Arrange lettuce leaves on individual plates, unmold aspic on to the lettuce leaves and garnish with onions and olives.

40

EGG AND CRESS SALAD (RECIPE PAGE 42) ▶

Egg and Cress Salad

Serves: 4
Cooking time: 10 minutes

   2 bunches of watercress
   3 eggs
   salt and pepper
   1 tablespoon lemon juice
   1 tablespoon wine vinegar
   ½ cup (125 ml) olive or salad oil
   ¼ teaspoon salt
   ¼ teaspoon black pepper

Wash, pat dry and chill the cress. Prick round end of each egg with a darning needle and place in a pan, cover with water bring to the boil and cook for 10 minutes. Drain, cool, shell and chill the eggs. Combine lemon juice, wine vinegar, oil, salt and black pepper in a jar. Cover and shake well until creamy. Chill.
Arrange cress in a salad bowl, sieve 2 of the eggs and sprinkle over the cress with salt and pepper. Sprinkle dressing over the salad and toss. Garnish with remaining egg cut into slices. Good with barbecued ham steak or pork chops.
(Illustrated on page 41.)

Stuffed Veal Shoulder

Serves: 4–6
Cooking time: 2–2¼ hours
Barbecue on the spit over medium coals

   3 lbs (1½ kg) boned shoulder of veal
   salt and pepper
   6 tablespoons butter, melted

Stuffing:
2 strips of bacon, minced
1 small onion, minced
2 sprigs parsley, minced
1½ cups soft breadcrumbs
½ teaspoon salt
pepper
2 teaspoons mixed herbs
½ cup (125 ml) white wine or water

Combine all ingredients for the stuffing in a bowl and mix well. Open out veal and season with salt and pepper. Spread with stuffing, roll and tie with stirring, then rub pepper into the skin. Thread a spit rod through the center of the meat and secure. Brush veal with butter and place on the spit over medium coals. Cook for 2–2¼ hours, until tender, basting with butter occasionally. Remove veal to a carving tray and allow to rest for 5 minutes, then slice and serve.

Liver Pâté Appetiser

Serves: 4–6
Cooking time: 25–30 minutes

   1 lb (500 g) chicken livers
   salted water
   ½ cup (125 g) butter
   1 large onion, finely chopped
   2 cloves garlic, crushed
   ¼ lb (125 g) bacon, chopped
   4 tablespoons cognac
   3 tablespoons port
   dash of Tabasco sauce
   salt and pepper
   ¼ teaspoon cayenne pepper
   ¼ teaspoon ground ginger
   ¼ teaspoon ground cloves
   ¼ cup (65 ml) scalded cream
   4 tablespoons extra butter

Trim chicken livers and place in a bowl, cover with salted water and set aside for 1 hour, then drain well and pat dry. Heat ½ cup butter in a pan, add chicken livers and cook 8–10 minutes, remove livers and place in a blender. To pan juices add onion, garlic and bacon and cook over low heat for 12–15 minutes, but do not brown. Stir in cognac, port, Tabasco sauce, salt, pepper, cayenne, ginger, cloves and scalded cream and cook 5 minutes, stirring constantly. Pour into the blender and whirl until mixture is smooth and fully blended. Spoon into individual bowls and chill until firm. Gently heat the extra butter over the pâté and refrigerate. Delicious as a first course with crunchy French bread, or pumpernickel.

Barbecued Chicken in Sour Cream

Serves: 4
Cooking time: 20–25 minutes
Barbecue on the grid over medium hot coals

4 chicken halves
1 cup (250 ml) sour cream
1 tablespoon lemon juice
1 teaspoon Worcestershire sauce
½ teaspoon paprika
salt and pepper
chopped parsley
Leek and Tomato Salad — see recipe page 54
Coleslaw Special — see recipe page 72

In a bowl combine sour cream, lemon juice, Worcestershire sauce, paprika, salt and pepper and mix well until blended, for a marinade. Place chicken halves in a glass or enamel dish and pour marinade over, baste, cover and chill 2½–3 hours, turning chicken and basting occasionally. Lift out chicken and drain, then place on the grid over medium hot coals and cook for 20–25 minutes, turning often and basting with the marinade. Serve hot with leek and tomato salad, coleslaw and crusty French bread.

Chicken Livers and Bacon Appetiser

Serves: 4–6
Cooking time: 12–15 minutes
Barbecue on skewers over medium hot coals

1 lb (500 g) chicken livers
½ lb (250 g) bacon
salt and pepper

Cut bacon into pieces, trim and rinse livers and pat dry. Sprinkle livers with salt and pepper and wrap each in a strip of bacon. Thread onto bamboo skewers and cook over medium hot coals for 12–15 minutes, turning frequently, until bacon is crisp and livers are cooked.

Barbecued Rolled Roast

Serves: 6–8
Cooking time: 1–1¼ hours for rare
Barbecue on the spit over medium hot coals

3 lbs (1½ kg) boned and rolled beef
seasoned pepper
Baked Potatoes — see recipe page 29
Pumpkin in Foil — see recipe page 51
Peas in Foil — see recipe page 51

Baste:
1 small onion, minced
1 teaspoon prepared mustard
1 tablespoon lemon juice
3 tablespoons red wine
4 tablespoons oil

Combine onion, mustard, lemon juice, wine and oil and mix until smooth. Insert the spit rod through the center of the meat and secure. Sprinkle meat with seasoned pepper and place on the spit over medium hot coals. Brush with the baste and cook for 1–1¼ hours for rare. Serve with potatoes, pumpkin and peas.

Foil Wrapped Potatoes

Serves: 4
Cooking time: 1 hour
Barbecue in foil over hot coals

4 large potatoes, scrubbed
1 tablespoon oil
3 tablespoons butter
6 tablespoons sour cream
chopped chives

Grease squares of doubled aluminium foil, dull side down, with oil and wrap potatoes, individually, and seal. Place on the grid over hot coals and cook for 1 hour, turning occasionally, until potatoes are soft, when lightly squeezed. Open top of foil, slash potatoes with a cross and open at top. Add butter, top with sour cream and sprinkle with chives. Serve with barbecued steak.

▲ PORK KEBABS ON CREAMED SPINACH (RECIPE PAGE 46)

▲ POTATO AND MUSSEL SALAD (RECIPE PAGE 46)

Sorrel Stuffed Mullet

Serves: 4–6
Cooking time: 1–1¼ hours
Barbecue in foil over medium hot coals

3 lbs (1½ kg) whole mullet, cleaned
¼ lb (125 g) sorrel leaves, chopped
3 tablespoons oil
salt and pepper
Saffron Rice Salad — see recipe page 85

Sorrel Sauce:
4 tablespoons oil
½ lb (250 g) sorrel leaves, chopped
2 egg yolks
1 teaspoon french mustard
salt and pepper

In a bowl, combine sorrel, oil, salt and pepper and mix well, then spoon into the cavity of the mullet and fasten with small skewers. Sprinkle fish with salt and pepper and place on greased, doubled aluminium foil, dull side down. Wrap the fish securely and place on the grid over medium hot coals and cook for 1–1¼ hours. Turn 2–3 times, while cooking.

To make sorrel sauce, heat 1 tablespoon of oil in a pan, add sorrel and soften over medium heat. When soft, mash to a purée, or blend in a blender. Spoon sorrel purée into the top of a double boiler and place over simmering water. Stir in egg yolks, mustard, salt and pepper, then stir in remaining oil, drop by drop, stirring constantly, until sauce is thickened. Remove from heat and pour into a flameproof bowl and set on the side of the barbecue to keep warm. Serve mullet with the sauce, and rice salad.

Pork Kebabs on Creamed Spinach

Serves: 4
Cooking time: 25–30 minutes
Barbecue on skewers over hot coals

1½ lbs (750 g) lean pork, cubed
3 medium onions, quartered

Marinade:
3 tablespoons oil
4 tablespoons lemon juice
3 tablespoons soy sauce
1 clove garlic, crushed
salt and seasoned pepper
1 teaspoon coriander

Creamed Spinach:
1 bunch spinach
½ cup (125 ml) boiling salted water
4 tablespoons butter
1 tablespoon flour
salt and pepper
¼ teaspoon sugar
½ cup (125 ml) milk
dash of nutmeg
½ teaspoon lemon juice
seasoned pepper
3 tablespoons thickened cream

Combine all ingredients for the marinade in a bowl and mix thoroughly, add pork cubes and baste, then set aside to marinate for 2½ hours, basting occasionally. Drain pork well and thread, alternately, with onion quarters, on skewers. Place over hot coals and cook for 25–30 minutes, until meat is tender, turning frequently and basting with the marinade.

Meanwhile, wash spinach well and place in a pan with the boiling salted water, cover and cook for 7–8 minutes to wilt. Drain thoroughly, then press through a sieve, or mince. Melt half the butter in a flameproof casserole, add spinach and cook, stirring, for 1–2 minutes. Mix flour, salt, pepper and sugar with a little milk to a smooth paste. Gradually stir in remaining milk, then stir into the spinach. Heat, then simmer gently for 15 minutes. Remove casserole to the side of the barbecue and keep warm. At serving, add remaining butter, in small pieces, nutmeg, lemon juice, seasoned pepper and

fold in cream and heat. Place spinach on warm plates and top with the pork kebabs.
(Illustrated on page 44.)

Potato and Mussel Salad

Serves: 4
Cooking time: 20 minutes

3 large potatoes
4 tablespoons white wine
1 tablespoon chopped chives
2 tablespoons chopped parsley
1 tablespoon chopped chervil
salt and pepper
3 tablespoons cider vinegar
6 tablespoons olive or salad oil
1 lb (500 g) shelled mussels, chilled
1 tablespoon chopped celery leaves

Place the potatoes in a pan of salted water, bring to the boil and cook for 15 minutes, strain and cool. Peel and slice the potatoes and place in a salad bowl, sprinkle with wine and toss gently. Add chives, parsley, chervil, salt and pepper. Mix vinegar and oil together in a jar and shake, then pour over the potatoes. Cover and chill for 2 hours. Add the mussels and celery leaves to the salad, toss gently, but thoroughly, and serve. Delicious with barbecued fish and hot crunchy bread.
(Illustrated on page 44.)

Ham and Cheese Appetisers

Serves: 4
Cooking time: 8–10 minutes
Barbecue on skewers over medium coals

8 slices ham loaf
prepared mustard
8 thin slices cheddar cheese
3 tablespoons butter
1 teaspoon honey

Spread mustard, sparingly, on ham slices and top, individually, with cheese slices. Roll up and thread onto bamboo skewers. Melt butter in a pan, stir in ½ teaspoon of mustard and the honey and mix. Brush mixture over ham rolls and cook over medium coals for 8–10 minutes, turning often and brushing with the butter mixture. Serve piping hot.

Barbecued Wine Pepper Steak

Serves: 6
Cooking time: 15–18 minutes
Barbecue on the grid over medium hot coals

6 thick sirloin steaks
coarsely ground black pepper
salt
4 tablespoons butter, melted
4 tablespoons olive oil
3 tablespoons red wine
3 tablespoons brandy
Mushrooms with Sour Cream — see
recipe page 58

Rub black pepper into steaks on both sides, pressing well into the meat with the heel of the hand, and sprinkle with salt. Place steaks on a greased grid over medium hot coals and cook for 15–18 minutes, for rare, turning often.
Combine butter, oil, wine and brandy in a bowl, mix well and heat. When steaks are almost cooked, brush with wine sauce on both sides. Before serving steaks, pour sauce over them and ignite. Serve with suggested salad.

Veal and Ham Kebabs

Serves: 4–6
Cooking time: 18–20 minutes
Barbecue on skewers over hot coals

¾ lb (375 g) lean veal, thinly sliced
¼ lb (125 g) cheddar cheese in slices
¼ lb (125 g) sliced ham
1 lemon thinly sliced
4 tablespoons butter, melted

Trim fat from veal and pound slices until very thin. Cover each veal slice with cheese, then ham and cheese again. Roll each veal slice tightly and fasten with cocktail sticks; chill for 1 hour. Cut veal rolls into 1″ (2½ cm) rounds and thread securely on skewers, alternately, with lemon slices. Brush with melted butter and cook over hot coals for 18–20 minutes, until tender, turning often and basting with butter.

Pork, Veal and Beef Terrine

Serves: 4–6
Cooking time: 2 hours
Oven: 180°C 350°F

½ lb (250 g) lean pork
½ lb (250 g) lean veal
½ lb (250 g) lean beef
3 teaspoons salt
seasoned pepper
½ teaspoon ground bay leaves
1 teaspoon thyme
2 tablespoons finely chopped parsley
1½ cups soft breadcrumbs
¼ cup milk
2 egg yolks
2 tablespoons brandy
8 strips of bacon

Grind the pork, veal and beef into a bowl, add salt, seasoned pepper, ground bay leaves, thyme and parsley. In a bowl, soak the breadcrumbs in milk until liquid is absorbed, then add to the meats with egg yolks and brandy. Mix together thoroughly with the fingers.
Grease a terrine and line with the bacon, add meat mixture and firm, bring bacon ends over the top of overlap. Cover and seal with a paste of plain flour and water mixed to a soft dough. Place terrine in a dish of hot water and cook in a moderate oven for 2 hours. Remove lid and press until cool, then cover and chill overnight. Cut in slices to serve.

Barbecued Chicken Paprika

Serves: 4
Cooking time: 30–35 minutes
Barbecue on grid over medium hot coals

> 2 × 1 lb (500 g) small chickens or Cornish Hens
> 4 tablespoons oil
> 4 tablespoons white wine
> 3 teaspoons paprika
> salt and pepper

In a bowl combine oil, wine, paprika, salt and pepper and mix thoroughly. Cut chickens in half and brush generously, on all sides, with this mixture. Sprinkle skin of chickens with more salt and place halves, bone side down, on the grid over medium hot coals. Cook for 10 minutes, turn, baste and cook another 10–15 minutes. Turn and baste and cook a further 10–15 minutes, until chicken is tender. Serve with crunchy French bread or Swiss stick.

Tangy Eggplant

Serves: 6
Serves: 12–15 minutes
Barbecue on the grid over medium hot coals

> 1 large egg plant
> ½ cup (125 ml) oil
> 3 tablespoons white vinegar
> pinch of oregano
> 1 teaspoon salt
> dash of seasoned pepper
> 1 clove garlic, crushed

In a jar combine oil, vinegar, oregano, salt, seasoned pepper and garlic, cover and shake to mix, then let stand for ¾ hour to blend for a baste. Cut eggplant into 6 wedges. Shake, baste, and brush eggplant wedges on all sides. Place on the grid over medium hot coals and cook for 12–15 minutes, turning and basting once or twice. Delicious with Spicy Leg of Lamb (see recipe page 83).

KEBABS OF BACON WRAPPED COD (RECIPE PAGE 50) ▶

Kebabs of Bacon Wrapped Cod

Serves: 4
Cooking time: 15–18 minutes
Barbecue on skewers over medium coals

1½ lbs (750 g) cod steaks
½ lb (250 g) bacon strips
salt and pepper
lemon wedges
Tomato and Sour Cream Salad — see recipe
    page 38
Old Fashioned Bread — see recipe page 85

Bone fish steaks, cut into even sized pieces and sprinkle with salt and pepper. Cut bacon strips in half and place each fish piece in half a strip and wrap. Thread kebabs securely on metal skewers and place over medium coals. Cook for 15–18 minutes, turning often, until bacon is crisp. Serve with lemon wedges, tomato salad and crusty hot bread.
(Illustrated on page 49.)

Avocado Appetiser

Serves: 4

2 ripe avocados
juice of 1 lemon
1 clove garlic, crushed
2 medium tomatoes, peeled
1 small white onion, peeled
½ small green bell pepper, seeded
1 stalk of white celery
salt and lemon pepper
3 tablespoons salad oil
1 tablespoon chopped parsley

Cut avocados in half, discard stones, scoop out the flesh into a bowl and sprinkle with lemon juice. In a blender place garlic, tomatoes, onion, bell pepper and celery and whirl until smooth. Add avocados with lemon juice, salt, lemon pepper, oil and parsley and blend. Spoon mixture into a bowl and chill. Serve with crusty bread.

Greek Salad

Serves: 6

1 head of crisp lettuce
1 small green bell pepper
1 small red bell pepper
6 radishes
4 scallions
2 tablespoons chopped parsley
2 medium tomatoes
10–12 black olives
¼ lb (125 g) feta cheese, crumbled
½ cup (125 ml) salad oil
3 tablespoons white vinegar
2 cloves garlic, crushed
salt and black pepper

In a salad bowl break the lettuce leaves into bite size pieces. Seed and thinly slice green and red bell peppers, quarter the radishes, chop the scallions and cut tomatoes into wedges. Add these ingredients to the lettuce with chopped parsley, olives and cheese. Combine the oil in a jar with vinegar, garlic, salt and freshly ground black pepper, cover and shake to mix. Pour this dressing over the salad and toss gently. Serve with barbecued meat.

Foil Wrapped Bananas

Serves: 4–6
Cooking time: 20–25 minutes
Barbecue in foil in glowing ashes

6 large bananas, peeled
3 tablespoons butter, melted
1 tablespoon sugar
dash of cinnamon

Brush bananas with butter and sprinkle with sugar and a little cinnamon. Wrap securely in doubled aluminium foil, dull side out, and bury in glowing ashes. Cook for 20–25 minutes, until tender. Serve hot as a dessert, or with barbecued meats.

Teriyaki Chicken

Serves: 4
Cooking time: 20–25 minutes
Barbecue on the grid over medium hot coals

8 chicken thighs
Teriyaki Marinade — see recipe page 88

Place chicken thighs in a dish, add marinade and baste. Cover and refrigerate for 3–4 hours, basting occasionally. Lift out chicken, drain and place on the grid over medium hot coals. Cook for 20–25 minutes, until tender, turning often and basting with the marinade.

Pumpkin in Foil

Serves: 4
Cooking time: 15–18 minutes
Barbecue in foil over medium coals

1 lb (500 g) pumpkin
salted water
2 tablespoons butter
salt and pepper

Peel and trim pumpkin and cut into pieces. Par-boil in a pan of salted water for 5 minutes and drain. Place pumpkin on doubled aluminium foil, dull side out, add butter, salt and pepper. Wrap securely and cook on the grid over medium coals for 10–12 minutes, until tender.

Peas in Foil

Serves: 4
Cooking time
Barbecue in foil over medium coals

2 cups frozen peas
1 teaspoon chopped mint
1 tablespoon butter
salt and pepper

Place peas on doubled aluminium foil, dull side out, add mint, butter, salt and pepper and wrap securely. Cook on the grid over medium coals for 10–12 minutes, until tender. Fresh peas can be used, but allow 4–5 minutes longer for cooking.

Barbecued Lamb on the Spit

Serves: 6–8
Cooking time: 2–2½ hours
Barbecue on the spit over medium hot coals

4 lbs (2 kg) leg of lamb
1 clove garlic, slivered
4 tablespoons dry breadcrumbs
1 tablespoon rosemary
1 tablespoon chopped parsley
1 clove garlic, crushed
salt and pepper
3 tablespoons butter, softened
4 tablespoons lemon juice
6–8 Foil Wrapped Potatoes — see
  recipe page 43
Ratatouille — see recipe page 35

Insert spit rod through the center of the meat, along the bone, and secure. Make slits in the skin and insert slivers of garlic. Combine breadcrumbs, rosemary, parsley, crushed garlic, salt, pepper, butter, and lemon juice and mix well. Press this mixture on the lamb on all sides, then let the meat marinate to absorb flavors for 2–2½ hours. Place rod on the spit over medium hot coals and cook for 2–2¼ hours, until tender.
Meanwhile prepare and cook foil wrapped potatoes and ratatouille. Lift leg of lamb to a carving board, remove rod and let meat rest 4–5 minutes, then carve and serve with vegetables.

Marinated Pork in Foil

Serves: 4
Cooking time: 35–40 minutes
Barbecue on grid over hot coals

1½ lbs (750 g) lean pork, cubed
¼ cup (125 ml) oil
1 teaspoon thyme
1 tablespoon chopped chives
1 tablespoon chopped parsley
1 clove garlic, crushed
1 small green bell pepper, finely sliced
2 tomatoes, finely chopped
salt and pepper

In a bowl combine oil, thyme, chives, parsley, garlic, bell pepper, salt and pepper and mix well. Add pork and baste, then set aside in a cool place to marinate for 2½–3 hours, basting occasionally. Cut doubled sheets of aluminium foil into large squares. With dull side down and sides turned up, spoon portions of pork and marinade onto foil, seal with a top twist, place on the grid over hot coals and cook for 35–40 minutes.

▼

Garlic Prawns

Serves: 4
Cooking time: 8–10 minutes
Barbecue in foil over smouldering coals

2 lbs (1 kg) prawns, shelled, retain tails
½ cup (125 g) butter
3 tablespoons oil
3 tablespoons lemon juice
2–3 cloves garlic, crushed
salt and lemon pepper
1 tablespoon finely chopped parsley

De-vein prawns and rinse in salted water, drain and place on doubled aluminium foil, formed into a dish. In a pan, combine butter, oil, lemon juice, garlic, salt, lemon pepper and parsley, heat and mix. Spread garlic butter over the prawns. Place foil dish on the grid over smouldering coals and cook for 8–10 minutes, until liquid is bubbling, turning prawns once or twice. Serve hot with crunchy bread.

Barbecued Sausages with Fresh Oysters

Serves: 4
Cooking time: 18–20 minutes
Barbecue on hot plate over hot coals

1 ½ lbs (750 g) thin sausages, pork or beef
water
4 teaspoons oil
3 tablespoons tomato catsup
salt and pepper
24 fresh oysters on the shell
lemon wedges

Place sausages in a pan and cover with cold water, bring to the boil and cook 2–3 minutes, then drain well. Brush sausages with oil and place on the hotplate over hot coals and cook for 18–20 minutes, turning often, until browned. Brush with catsup and serve with the fresh oysters, lemon wedges, salt and pepper. Goes well with crunchy bread, washed down with dry white wine.

Anchovy Stuffed Prawn Appetisers

Serves: 4–6
Cooking time: 12–15 minutes
Barbecue on skewers over medium hot coals

12 large fresh prawns
12 anchovy fillets
6 bacon strips
Basic Lemon Baste — see recipe page 88

Shell and de-vein prawns. Make a deep cut, lengthwise, down the back of each prawn and insert one anchovy. Split bacon strips in half, wrap each piece around a prawn and thread onto bamboo skewers. Cook over medium hot coals for 12–15 minutes, turning frequently, until bacon is crisp. Meanwhile, prepare and heat the baste, remove kebabs from the fire, brush with the hot baste and serve hot.

Goddess Salad

Serves: 6

1 head of lettuce

Dressing:
1¼ cups (300 ml) mayonnaise
4 anchovies, crushed
2 tablespoons chopped parsley
2 tablespoons chopped chives
1 clove garlic, crushed
1 tablespoon tarragon vinegar
1 tablespoon lemon juice
salt and pepper
4 tablespoons thick sour cream

Wash the lettuce leaves and pat dry, then roll in a towel and crisp in the refrigerator for 1 hour. Meanwhile, in a blender place mayonnaise, anchovies, parsley, chives, garlic, vinegar, lemon juice, salt and pepper and blend for 2−3 minutes until creamy. Pour mixture into a bowl, stir in sour cream and mix well, then chill for at least 15 minutes.
Tear lettuce leaves into bite size pieces and place in a salad bowl, add dressing, and toss.

Leek and Tomato Salad

Serves: 4

6 crisp lettuce leaves
2 medium tomatoes, cut into wedges
2 leeks, white parts only, thinly sliced
½ cup (125 ml) French Dressing — see recipe
  page 92
½ teaspoon prepared mustard
1 tablespoon finely chopped parsley
½ teaspoon chopped basil

Tear lettuce leaves into bite size pieces and place in a salad bowl, add tomato wedges and sliced leeks. Combine dressing and mustard and mix well, then pour over the salad and toss well. Sprinkle salad with parsley and basil and serve.

Teriyaki Lamb Kebabs

Serves: 4−6
Cooking time: 18−20 minutes
Barbecue on skewers over hot coals

1½ lbs (750 g) lean, boneless lamb, cubed
Soy and Ginger Marinade — see recipe page 88
2 medium onions
1 small green bell pepper
1 small red bell pepper

Place lamb cubes in a glass or enamel dish, add marinade, baste and set aside for 1−1¼ hours to marinate. Meanwhile, quarter the onions; seed the bell peppers and cut into chunks.
Drain the meat. Pour marinade into a pan and heat to bubbly on the side of the fire. Thread lamb on skewers, alternately, with onion quarters and pepper chunks. Cook over hot coals for 18−20 minutes, until tender, turning often and brushing with the heated marinade.

Meat Ball Appetisers

Serves: 8−10
Cooking time: 20 minutes
Cook in a pan over medium hot coals

1 lb (500 g) top round steak
1 medium onion
salt and pepper
1 egg
¾ cup soft breadcrumbs
1 tablespoon catsup
1 teaspoon Worcestershire sauce
1 tablespoon chopped parsley
2 tablespoons water
flour
2 tablespoons oil
1 tablespoon margarine

Grind meat and onion and place on a large dish. Add salt, pepper, egg, breadcrumbs, tomato and Worcestershire sauces, parsley and water. Mix together thoroughly, using hands, then shape into bite size balls and roll in flour. In a heavy pan heat oil and margarine, add enough meat balls to cover the base of the pan and cook over medium hot coals, turning often, until brown on all sides. Remove meat balls from pan into a dish and keep warm, until all the meat balls are cooked. Insert a cocktail stick into each meatball and serve with bowls of catsup, chutney or mustard sauce.

Trim and discard crusts from bread, break slices into small pieces into a dish, add milk and set aside for 5 minutes to soak. Place fish roe in a bowl and mash until smooth, then mix in onion and garlic. Squeeze all moisture from the bread and blend with the fish roe. Add lemon juice and oil, alternately, in small amounts, beating well until the mixture is very smooth, then strain through a fine sieve into a small bowl and chill. Sprinkle with parsley and garnish with olives. Serve with crackers.

Artichoke Salad

Cooking time: 35 minutes

6 artichokes
boiling salted water
2 medium onions, chopped
2 bay leaves
3 peppercorns
½ cup (125 ml) French Dressing — see recipe
    page 92

Wash artichokes and trim, then plunge into a pan of boiling salted water, then add onions, bay leaves, and peppercorns. Cover and simmer for 30–35 minutes, until leaves are loose. Remove artichokes, cool and chill. Pour dressing over artichokes and serve.

Caesar Salad

Serves: 4–6
Cooking time: 10 minutes

1 medium head of lettuce
¼ cup oil
2 cloves garlic, halved
2 cups bread cubes
small can of anchovy fillets, drained
pinch of dry mustard
½ teaspoon salt
dash of seasoned pepper
1 clove garlic, crushed
1 teaspoon Worcestershire sauce
2 tablespoons tarragon vinegar
1 tablespoon lemon juice
¼ cup olive or salad oil
2 eggs boiled for 2 minutes
3 tablespoons grated Parmesan cheese

Taramasalata (Fish Roe) Appetiser

Serves: 6–8

¼ lb (125 g) tarama (fish roe)
4 slices white bread
1 tablespoon milk
1 small white onion, minced
1 clove garlic, crushed
1 tablespoon lemon juice
4 tablespoon olive or salad oil
1 tablespoon chopped parsley
stuffed olives
crackers

Separate lettuce into leaves, wash and dry, then chill for 40–45 minutes. Tear leaves into bite size pieces and place in a salad bowl.
Heat oil in a pan, add garlic and cook 2–3 minutes, add bread cubes and sauté until golden brown, then remove and drain on paper towels and set aside for croutons.
Mash anchovies and mix with mustard, salt, seasoned pepper and garlic. Spoon into a blender, add Worcestershire sauce, tarragon vinegar, lemon juice and olive oil and blend until creamy, then pour over the lettuce.
Spoon lightly cooked eggs into a bowl, beat well then pour over the salad. Sprinkle cheese and croutons over the lettuce, toss and serve immediately as a first course, or with barbecued steak.

Cabbage and Bacon Salad

Serves: 4

> 5–6 white cabbage leaves
> ½ lb (250 g) thick bacon or salt pork, diced
> seasoned pepper
> ½ cup (125 ml) Coleslaw Dressing — see
>   recipe page 90

Cook the bacon in a pan until crisp and drain well. Shred the cabbage leaves and place in a salad bowl, add bacon and sprinkle with pepper. Serve with the dressing.

▼

Prosciutto and Melon Appetisers

Serves: 4

> 2 ripe cantaloupe, chilled
> 4 tablespoons port
> ½ lb (250 g) prosciutto, sliced paper thin

Cut melons in half, lengthwise, and remove seeds and membranes. With a melon baller, scoop out the flesh from the melon halves into balls, taking care not to break the melon skin. Return melon balls to half shells and sprinkle with port. Top with rolled prosciutto slices, and serve.

ENGLISH BLOOD PUDDING AND BRATWURST BARBECUED (RECIPE PAGE 58) ▶

English Blood Pudding and Bratwurst

Serves: 4
Cooking time: 15–18 minutes
Barbecue on a grid over medium coals

    1 lb (500 g) English blood pudding
    1 lb (500 g) bratwurst
    3 cooking apples
    ½ cup (125 ml) water
    2 teaspoons sugar

Peel, core and slice apples and place in a heavy pan with water. Cover and bring to the boil over coals and cook 8–10 minutes, add sugar and cook a further 4–5 minutes, stirring and mashing, until apples are almost pulp; draw pan to the side of barbecue, cover and keep apples warm.
Meanwhile, prick bratwurst in several places and cook in water for 3–4 minutes, then drain. Arrange blood pudding and bratwurst on a grid and cook over medium coals until skins are crisp, turn and crisp other side. Slice into portions and serve with cooked apples.
(Illustrated on page 57.)

Barbecued Cheese Burgers

Serves: 4
Cooking time: 15–18 minutes
Barbecue on the grid over hot coals

    1½ lbs (750 g) ground beef
    1 medium onion, finely chopped
    1 clove garlic, crushed
    1 teaspoon salt
    sprinkle of seasoned pepper
    1½ cups grated cheddar cheese
    ¼ cup (65 ml) red wine or water
    2 tablespoons tomato catsup
    dash of Tabasco sauce
    1 tablespoon oil
    Special Cucumber Salad — see recipe page 22

On a dish combine meat, onion, garlic, salt, savoury pepper, grated cheese and wine or water and mix well. Shape into 8 patties. Mix tomato and Tabasco sauces with the oil and brush over the meat. Place patties on the grid over hot coals and cook for 15–18 minutes, turning often and basting with the sauce. Serve hot with cucumber salad and cheese puffs.

Mushrooms with Sour Cream

Serves: 4

    ¾ lb (375 g) button mushrooms
    ½ cup (125 ml) light sour cream
    3 tablespoons milk
    1 teaspoon lemon juice
    salt and pepper
    1 tablespoon finely chopped chives

Wipe mushrooms and trim stems, do not peel, slice thinly and evenly. In a salad bowl, combine sour cream, milk, lemon juice, salt and pepper and mix well. Add mushrooms and baste, sprinkle with chives and serve.

Pickled Beets

Serves: 10–12
Cooking time: 1½–1¾ hours
Oven: 180°C   350°F

    2 bunches of large beets
    5 cups (1¼ quarts) malt vinegar
    1 teaspoon ground mace
    1 teaspoon ground allspice
    1 teaspoon ground cloves
    1 teaspoon ground cinnamon
    6 peppercorns, bruised
    2 teaspoons salt

Place vinegar in an enamel pan. Combine mace, allspice, cloves, cinnamon and peppercorns in a double muslin bag, tie securely and lower into the vinegar. Bring liquid to the boil, lower heat, cover and simmer gently for 3–4 minutes. Remove pan from heat and allow to stand for 2 hours, then lift out spices.

Meanwhile, wash beets carefully, leave some stalk on each beet, dry, place in a baking pan and cook in a moderate oven for 1½–1¾ hours, until tender. Remove from heat and allow beets to cool, then trim, slip off skins and slice into jars, packing firmly. Heat spiced vinegar, add salt and dissolve, then pour over beets to cover. Seal jars securely and wait at least 10 days before using.

Picnic Quiche

Serves: 4–6
Looking time: 40–45 minutes
Oven: 190°C 375°F

1 medium eggplant, peeled and diced
3 tablespoons oil
1 medium onion, chopped
salt and seasoned pepper
1 teaspoon ground bay leaves
2 large tomatoes, peeled and chopped
¼ lb (125 g) ham, diced
2 eggs, beaten
½ cup (125 ml) cream
2 tablespoons grated cheddar cheese
1 tablespoon finely chopped parsley
9″ (23 cm) pie shell
1 tablespoon butter

Place eggplant in a bowl, sprinkle with salt and set aside for 30 minutes, then rinse under running water, drain and pat dry. Heat oil in a pan, add eggplant and cook, stirring, until tender, then lift out and place in a bowl. To pan juices add onion and sauté until transparent, stir in salt, seasoned pepper, ground bay leaves and tomatoes. Cook until mixture is thick, stirring often, then add to the eggplant with the ham. Beat eggs and cream together in a bowl, stir in cheese and parsley, then fold into the eggplant mixture.

Turn mixture into the pie shell, dot with butter and cook in a moderately hot oven for 30–35 minutes, until set. Remove quiche from oven, cook and chill.

Banana and Scallop Kebabs

Serves: 6
Cooking time: 15–18 minutes
Barbecue on skewers over hot coals

6 firm bananas, cut in thick slices
1 lb (500 g) scallops
4 tablespoons lemon juice
4 tablespoons butter, melted

Combine lemon juice and melted butter in a bowl, mix well and keep warm on the side of the barbecue. Thread banana slices and scallops, alternately, onto skewers and brush liberally with warm lemon butter baste. Place kebabs over hot coals and cook for 15–18 minutes, turning often and basting. At serving brush with remaining baste.

Pepper Pork Chops

Serves: 4
Cooking time: 18–20 minutes
Barbecue on the grid over medium coals

4 pork loin chops
2 tablespoons freshly ground black pepper
4 tablespoons butter, melted
sprinkle of salt
Glazed Pineapple Rings — see recipe page 34

Sprinkle chops with black pepper on both sides and press in well with the heel of the hand. Brush with butter and lightly sprinkle with salt. Place on the grid over medium coals and cook for 18–20 minutes, until tender, turning often and brushing with butter. Serve with pineapple rings.

Meanwhile cook beans in a pan of boiling salted water for 10 minutes, strain and place in a flameproof casserole with butter, garlic, salt and seasoned pepper. Cover and cook over coals for 10–12 minutes. Serve the beans with the chicken and saffron rice salad.

Barbecued Veal in Foil

Serves: 6
Cooking time: 30–35 minutes
Barbecue on grid over medium hot coals

*2 lbs (1 kg) veal steak, or 6 pieces
    1" (2½ cm) thick
½ lb (250 g) mushrooms
¼ lb (125 g) bacon strips
1 tablespoon chopped parsley
salt and seasoned pepper
⅓ cup (85 ml) heavy cream*

Cut edges of meat to prevent curling. Slice mushrooms in half. Coarsely chop the bacon strips. Place each veal steak on a doubled piece of aluminium foil, dull side down, and turn the sides of the foil up. Place the mushrooms and bacon on top of the meat. Sprinkle with parsley, salt and seasoned pepper, then pour cream over each steak. Seal foil securely. Place on the grid over medium hot coals and cook for 30–35 minutes, until veal is tender. Turn once during cooking. Open top of the foil and serve.

▼

Chicken Halves with Beans

Serves: 4
Cooking time: 30–35 minutes
Barbecue on the grid over medium hot coals

*4 chicken halves
1 teaspoon dry mustard
1 tablespoon curry powder
1 teaspoon salt
3 tablespoons white wine
½ cup honey
¾ lb (375 g) beans, trimmed
boiling salted water
4 tablespoons butter
1 clove garlic, crushed
salt and seasoned pepper
Saffron Rice Salad — see recipe page 85*

Mix mustard, curry powder and salt with wine until smooth, then stir in honey. Place chicken halves on the grid over medium hot coals and cook for 20 minutes, turning once, then baste, generously, with the honey mixture and cook a further 10–15 minutes, until tender, turning and basting frequently while cooking.

KEBABS ESPAGNOLE (RECIPE PAGE 62) ▶

Kebabs Espagnole

Serves: 4
Cooking time: 10–12 minutes
Barbecue on skewers over medium coals

    2 pepperoni sausages
    5 thickly sliced bacon strips
    1 large green bell pepper
    1 large red bell pepper
    1 medium tomato
    3 tablespoons oil

Cut sausages into thick slices. Slice each bacon strip into 4 or 5 pieces. Seed both bell peppers and cut into chunks. Slice tomato thickly.
Thread sausages, bacon, green and red peppers and tomato slices, alternately, on metal skewers. Brush with oil and cook over medium coals for 10–12 minutes, turning often and basting with oil, until bacon is crisp.
(Illustrated on page 61.)

Kebabs Piraeus

Serves: 6
Cooking time: 12–15 minutes
Barbecue on skewers over medium coals

    2 lbs (1 kg) firm, white, fish fillets
    1 large green bell pepper, seeded
    6 bay leaves, halved
    2 medium tomatoes
    6 button mushrooms
    1 lemon, cut in wedges

Marinade:
3 tablespoons oil
¼ cup white wine
1 tablespoon lemon juice
½ teaspoon oregano
1 clove garlic, crushed
1 small onion, grated
salt and pepper

Make the marinade by mixing together oil, wine, lemon juice, oregano, garlic, onion, salt and pepper in a bowl. Cut fish into 1″ (2½ cm) cubes, place in a glass dish and pour marinade over cubes. Allow to marinate at least 2 hours, turning and basting occasionally.
Cut pepper and tomatoes into chunks, trim and wipe mushrooms. Drain fish cubes and thread on to skewers, alternately, with bay leaves, pepper and tomato chunks. Top each skewer with a mushroom. Place kebabs over medium coals and cook 12–15 minutes, turning often and basting with remaining marinade. Serve with lemon wedges.

Suckling Pig on the Spit

Serves: 12–14
Cooking time: 6–6½ hours
Barbecue on the spit over medium hot coals

    1 plump piglet, about 12 lbs (6 kg), dressed
    olive oil
    salt
    2 teaspoons dry mustard
    3 tablespoons flour
    ½ teaspoon pepper
    1 red apple
    2 raisins

Fruit and Onion Stuffing:
3 cooking apples, cored, unpeeled, cut in
    wedges
¼ cup brown sugar
¼ cup white wine
¼ cup water
2 medium onions, roughly chopped
¾ cup prunes, pitted
¾ cup dried apricots, soaked
½ teaspoon cinnamon
¼ teaspoon nutmeg
¾ cup (185 ml) red wine

Cook apples, sugar, wine and water together in a pan until almost tender, stirring occasionally. Add onions, prunes, apricots, cinnamon, nutmeg and wine and simmer 4–5 minutes.
Clean and wipe the piglet thoroughly, score the skin and place a ball of foil in the mouth. Fill the cavity with stuffing and sew to close. Skewer the

hind legs backwards and the forelegs forwards. Thread the spit rod through the center of the piglet, tail to head, and secure. Brush with oil and sprinkle well with salt. Place on the spit over medium hot coals and cook for 6–6½ hours, until tender. Place a baking dish or foil tray on coals beneath the meat to catch drippings and prevent flaring. Baste with drippings every 15 minutes. Towards the end of the cooking, mix mustard, flour and pepper together and sprinkle meat well. Lift piglet from the spit to a carving tray, remove rod and allow meat to rest for 5 minutes. Remove foil from the mouth and replace with a red apple and place a raisin in each eye. The piglet can also be cooked in a moderate oven for 3 hours, then transferred to the spit for final 3–3½ hours.

Greek Lamb Patties

Serves: 4–6
Cooking time: 18–20 minutes
Barbecue on the grid over hot coals

  1½ lb (750 g) lean lamb, finely ground
  1 medium onion, minced
  ¼ lb (125 g) pine nuts
  ½ teaspoon nutmeg
  salt and pepper
  3 tablespoons oil
  1 tablespoon white wine
  1 teaspoon chopped mint
  pinch of thyme
  Tomato and Sour Cream Salad — see
    recipe page 38

In a bowl combine ground lamb, onion, pine nuts, nutmeg, salt and pepper and mix thoroughly, add a little water if mixture is too dry, then shape into 8 patties. In a jar, mix oil, wine, mint, thyme, salt and pepper, cover and shake well. Brush patties with this baste, place on the grid over hot coals and cook for 18–20 minutes, turning often and basting. Serve hot with tomato salad and crusty bread.

Pâté Stuffed Mushrooms with Bacon

Serves: 8–10
Cooking time: 15–20 minutes
Cook in a pan over medium hot coals

  1 lb (500 g) evenly sized mushrooms
  salt and pepper
  ½ lb (250 g) chicken liver pâté
  ½ lb (250 g) bacon, cut into pieces
  2 tablespoons butter

Wipe mushrooms and remove stems. Sprinkle mushrooms with salt and pepper and fill each cap with pâté. In a large, heavy pan cook the bacon pieces over medium hot coals, until crisp. Remove pan from heat, lift out bacon, drain on paper towels and keep warm. To pan juices add butter and melt. Arrange mushroom caps, pâté side up, in the pan and cook for 6–8 minutes, turn caps carefully and cook a further 6–8 minutes. Serve bacon and mushrooms as a hot appetiser.

Prune and Cream Cheese Appetisers

Serves: 4–6
Cooking time: 12–15 minutes
Barbecue on skewers over medium hot coals

  24 large prunes
  ¼ lb (125 g) cream cheese
  ½ lb (250 g) bacon strips
  1 teaspoon paprika

Pit the prunes, cut the bacon into 24 strips and blend cream cheese and paprika together. Stuff each prune with the cheese mixture and wrap with a strip of bacon. Thread onto bamboo skewers and cook over medium hot coals for 12–15 minutes, turning often, until bacon is crisp. Serve hot.

Red Cabbage and Apples

Serves: 4–6
Cooking time: 1–1¼ hours

½ red cabbage, shredded
3 tablespoons butter
1 large onion, finely chopped
3 cooking apples, peeled, cored and quartered
½ teaspoon salt
3 tablespoons boiling water
2 bay leaves
3 tablespoons red wine
3 tablespoons brown sugar

Soak cabbage in a bowl of cold water for 10–15 minutes, then drain. Melt the butter in a large pan, add onion and sauté for 2–3 minutes, add moist cabbage, cover and simmer gently for 10–12 minutes. Add apples, salt, boiling water and bay leaves. Cover and simmer gently for 45–50 minutes, until tender and moisture is absorbed. Stir in wine and sugar, cover and simmer a further 8–10 minutes. Discard bay leaves and serve hot.

Kebabs of Curried Lamb

Serves: 4–6
Cooking time: 20–25 minutes
Barbecue on skewers over hot coals

1 lb (500 g) lean lamb, cubed
3 medium onions, cut in wedges
3 green apples
juice of 1 lemon
4–6 sprigs of rosemary

Marinade:
2 teaspoons ground ginger
2 teaspoons curry powder
3 teaspoons soy sauce
3 tablespoons honey
4 tablespoons white wine

Combine ginger, curry powder, soy sauce, honey and wine in a pan and heat, stirring, then allow to cool, for a marinade. Place lamb cubes in a glass dish, add marinade and baste, set aside for at least 1 hour, basting occasionally. Peel and core apples and cut into quarters, place in a glass dish, add lemon juice and baste. Drain lamb, but reserve marinade. Drain apples. Thread lamb, onions, apples and rosemary, alternately, on skewers and cook over hot coals for 18–20 minutes, until tender, turning often and brushing with the marinade.

Marinated Fillet Steak

Serves: 4
Cooking time: 15–18 minutes
Barbecue on the grid over medium hot coals

4 thick slices of fillet steak
3 tablespoons butter, melted
Green Bean and Onion Salad — see
  recipe page 80

Marinade:
4 tablespoons red wine
4 tablespoons wine vinegar
1 teaspoon ground bay leaves
salt and pepper

Combine wine, vinegar, ground bay leaves, salt and pepper in a bowl and mix well for the marinade. Place steaks in a shallow glass or enamel dish and pour marinade over. Set aside in a cool place for 3½–4 hours, turning and basting once or twice. Return dish to room temperature 1 hour before cooking. Lift out meat and pat dry, but reserve marinade. Brush steaks with butter, place on the grid over medium hot coals and cook for 7–8 minutes on each side, for rare.
Meanwhile, pour marinade into a heavy pan and cook over coals to reduce to ¼ cup (65 ml). Serve steaks with reduced marinade sauce, accompanied by green bean salad, crunchy French bread and red wine.

Barbecued Nutty Hamburgers

Serves: 6–8
Cooking time: 18–20 minutes
Barbecue on the grid over hot coals

3 lbs (1½ kg) ground beef
2 eggs
2 medium onions, minced
¾ cup finely chopped cashew nuts
salt and pepper
12 pineapple rings, fresh or canned
4 ripe tomatoes, thickly sliced
chopped parsley
Watercress and Mushroom Salad — see
  recipe page 29
Garlic Bread — see recipe page 85

In a bowl combine meat, eggs, onions, nuts, salt and pepper and mix thoroughly. Shape into 12 patties and place on the grid over hot coals. Cook for 18–20 minutes, turning 3–4 times.
Meanwhile barbecue pineapple rings, tomato slices and for 3–4 minutes on each side. Arrange pineapple rings on individual plates, add hamburgers and top with tomato slice. Secure the layers with cocktail sticks, sprinkle with parsley and serve with suggested salad and bread.

Kebabs of Pork and Rosemary

Serves: 4
Cooking time: 25–30 minutes
Barbecue on skewers over hot coals

 1½ lbs (750 g) lean pork, cubed
 4 tablespoons vinegar
 4 tablespoons oil
 sprigs of fresh rosemary
 salt and seasoned pepper

In a bowl combine vinegar, oil, rosemary, salt and seasoned pepper and mix well. Add pork and baste, then set aside in a cool place to marinate for 2½–3 hours, basting occasionally. Remove meat and drain, but reserve marinade. Thread pork cubes on to metal skewers and cook over hot coals for 25–30 minutes, turning often. Baste with marinade 3 or 4 times during cooking.

Apple and Beet Salad

Serves: 4

 4 unpeeled apples, cored and diced
 4 cooked beets, peeled and diced
 2 hard boiled eggs, coarsley chopped
 1 tablespoon chopped parsley
 salt and pepper
 ½ cup (125 ml) French Dressing — see
   recipe page 92
 ½ cup chopped walnuts

In a salad bowl combine apples, beets, eggs, parsley, salt and pepper, add dressing and toss gently. Chill for at least 1 hour, then sprinkle with chopped walnuts and serve.

ANCHOVY TOPPED ENTRECÔTES (RECIPE PAGE 68) ▶

Anchovy Topped Entrecôtes

Serves: 4
Cooking time: 30–35 minutes for rare
Barbecue on grid over medium hot coals

> 2 lbs (1 kg) boned rib steaks (4)
> 32 anchovy fillets
> 2 cloves garlic, crushed
> dash of seasoned pepper
> 1 tablespoon oil
> 1 tablespoon capers

Mash half the anchovies on a plate with the crushed garlic and sesoned pepper to a paste. Place the plate at the side of the barbecue, to gently warm.
Trim steaks and brush with oil on both sides, then place on a grid over medium glowing coals. Cook for 30–35 minutes, turning 3–4 times. Five minutes before steaks are ready, spread anchovy paste thickly over each steak and garnish with capers and remaining anchovy fillets. Serve entrecôtes on hot plates, with crusty bread.
(Illustrated on page 67.)

Quail in Ashes

Serves: 4
Cooking time: 35–40 minutes
Barbecue in hot glowing ashes

> 4 plump quails, cleaned and dressed
> salt and pepper
> ½ lb (250 g) white grapes, seeded
> 6 tablespoons butter
> grape leaves
> 4 large thin slices of fat pork
> Stuffed Lettuce — see recipe page 77

Rub the cavity of each quail with salt and pepper, insert 6–7 grapes and close the opening with skewers. Brush butter over each bird, sprinkle with salt and pepper and wrap in slices of pork and grape leaves, then in 2 thicknesses of buttered paper. Bury the quails in hot ashes of the barbecue and cook for 35–40 minutes. As ashes cool, renew with hot ashes on all sides. Lift out the birds, unwrap and serve at once, with stuffed lettuce and hot crunchy bread rolls.

Marinated Lamb Kebabs

Serves: 6
Cooking time: 20 minutes
Barbecue on skewers over hot coals

> 2 lbs (1 kg) lean lamb, cubed
> ½ cup rice
> boiling salted water
> 14 oz (440 g) can concentrated tomato soup
> ½ cup (125 ml) white wine
> chopped parsley
>
> **Marinade:**
> ½ cup (125 ml) oil
> 1 small onion, finely chopped
> 1 clove garlic, crushed
> ¼ teaspoon saffron
> ½ teaspoon ground cinnamon
> ½ teaspoon ground caraway
> ½ teaspoon coriander
> 1 teaspoon salt
> seasoned pepper

Make the marinade by combining all ingredients and mixing well. Place the lamb cubes in a glass bowl and add the marinade. Set aside for 3–3½ hours, stirring and basting occasionally. Lift out lamb cubes and drain well, then thread onto skewers. Place over hot coals and cook for 18–20 minutes, until tender, turning and basting often, with the marinade.
Meanwhile, cook rice in a pan of boiling salted water for 15 minutes, drain in a colander and wash thoroughly. Place colander over simmering water to heat rice. Mix soup and wine in a pan, heat and simmer 3–4 minutes.
Serve lamb kebabs with rice, topped with thick tomato soup and sprinkled with parsley.

Barbecued Lamb Shanks

Serves: 4
Cooking time: 30–35 minutes
Barbecue on the grid over medium hot coals

4 lamb shanks, trimmed
1 teaspoon dry mustard
½ teaspoon ground ginger
pinch of mace
3 teaspoons brown sugar, firmly packed
1 tablespoon lemon juice
3 tablespoons soy sauce
½ cup (125 ml) pineapple juice
4 tablespoons olive or salad oil

Combine mustard, ginger, mace, brown sugar and lemon juice in a bowl, and mix until smooth, stir in soy sauce, pineapple juice and oil and blend. Place lamb shanks in a glass or enamel dish, add marinade, baste and set aside for 2–2¼ hours to marinate, basting occasionally, then drain meat well. Pour marinade into a pan and heat until bubbly on the side of the fire.
Place meat on the grid over medium hot coals and cook for 30–35 minutes, until tender, turning often and brushing with the marinade.

Barbecued Steak in Ginger Marinade

Serves: 6
Cooking time: 15–18 minutes
Barbecue on the grid over hot coals

6 thick sirloin steaks, trimmed
4 tablespoons butter, melted
Special Cucumber Salad — see recipe page 22

Marinade:
4 tablespoons soy sauce
½ cup (125 ml) pineapple juice
4 tablespoons dry sherry
1 tablespoon ground ginger
1 clove garlic, crushed
½ teaspoon salt

Combine soy sauce, pineapple juice and sherry in a bowl with ginger, garlic and salt and mix until smooth. Place steaks in a large, shallow glass or enamel dish, pour marinade over and let stand in a cool place for 3½–4 hours, basting occasionally. Drain meat and pat dry. Brush steaks with butter on all sides, place on the grid over hot coals and cook for 6–8 minutes on each side, for rare, basting often with butter. Meanwhile pour marinade into a heavy pan and cook over coals to reduce to ¼ cup (65 ml). Serve steaks with reduced marinade, accompanied by cucumber salad and hot crunchy bread.

Marinated Seafood Kebabs

Serves: 4–6
Cooking time: 12–15 minutes
Barbecue on skewers over medium coals

2 lbs (1 kg) shelled and de-veined fresh prawns
½ lb (250 g) fish fillets, cubed
1 cup (250 ml) boiling water
½ cup coconut
2 teaspoons soy sauce
1 clove garlic, crushed
salt and pepper
2 teaspoons ground cumin
1 tablespoon lemon juice
Tomato and Mint Salad — see recipe page 17
Garlic Bread — see recipe page 85

Remove boiling water from heat, add coconut and infuse for 6–8 minutes, then pour into a blender and whirl 2–3 minutes. Strain into a bowl through muslin to extract coconut milk. Add soy sauce, garlic, salt, pepper, cumin and lemon juice and mix well. Add prawns and fish to the mixture and marinade for 1–1¼ hours, stirring and basting occasionally. Drain seafood and thread, alternately, on skewers. Place on the grid over medium coals and cook 12–15 minutes, turning often. Baste with the marinade while cooking. Serve hot with tomato and mint salad and garlic bread.

Bacon Wrapped Shrimp Kebabs

Serves: 4
Cooking time: 12–15 minutes
Barbecue on skewers over hot embers

1½ lbs (750 g) fresh shrimp
¼ lb (125 g) bacon strips
2 tablespoons butter, melted
3 tablespoons lemon juice
3 tablespoons mayonnaise
1 tablespoon cream, whipped
2 tablespoons finely chopped chives
chopped parsley

Shell and de-vein the shrimp. Cut each bacon strip into 3 or 4 pieces. Wrap each shrimp in a piece of bacon and thread onto metal skewers. Mix together butter and half the lemon juice for a baste and brush over the kebabs, then place over hot embers. Cook, turning and basting, for 12–15 minutes, until bacon is crisp and shrimp are red. Sprinkle with chives. Combine mayonnaise and whipped cream and mix well, sprinkle with chives and parsley and serve with the kebabs.

▼

Lamb Chops in Tarragon Oil

Serves: 4
Cooking time: 12–15 minutes
Barbecue on the grid over medium hot coals

8 loin lamb chops
6 tablespoons oil
1 tablespoon chopped fresh tarragon
salt and pepper
4 medium tomatoes
grated Parmesan cheese

Combine oil and tarragon in a bowl and mix well, brush chops on both sides with the mixture and place in a shallow glass or enamel dish, sprinkle with salt and pepper and set aside for 30 minutes. Brush chops again, place on the grid over medium hot coals and cook for 12–15 minutes, until tender, turning often and basting. Meanwhile, cut tomatoes in half, place cut side up on the barbecue grid and cook for 3 minutes, turn tomatoes and cook a further 3 minutes. Sprinkle tomatoes with cheese and serve with the chops, lettuce salad with French dressing.

Crab and Melon Salad

Serves: 4

14 oz (440 g) can of crabmeat, chilled
1 medium cantaloupe
3 large crisp lettuce leaves, shredded
½ cup (125 ml) French Dressing — see
* recipe page 92*

Drain and flake the crabmeat. Cut melon in quarters, remove seeds and membranes and scoop out the flesh in pieces. Place lettuce in the base of a salad bowl and add crabmeat and melon pieces. Sprinkle French dressing over and serve with barbecued fish.

Marinated Drumsticks

Serves: 4
Cooking time: 20–25 minutes
Barbecue on the grid over medium hot coals

8 chicken drumsticks
Herbs and Wine Marinade — see recipe page 87

Place drumsticks in a dish and add marinade. Cover and set aside for 2–2½ hours, basting occasionally. Lift out drumsticks, drain and place on the grid over medium hot coals. Cook for 20–25 minutes, until tender, turning often and basting with the marinade.

Honeyed Chicken Halves

Serves: 4
Cooking time: 20–25 minutes
Barbecue on the grid over medium hot coals

4 chicken halves
salt and pepper
1 teaspoon dry mustard
1 teaspoon white wine
3 tablespoons honey

Sprinkle chicken halves with salt and pepper. Mix mustard and wine together in a bowl, until smooth, then stir in honey to blend. Place chicken on the grid over medium hot coals and brush with honey mixture. Cook for 20–25 minutes, until tender, turning often and basting.

Spiced Fish

Serves: 4
Cooking time: 10–12 minutes
Oven: 180°C 350°F

1 lb (500 g) fish fillets
1 medium onion, sliced in rings
4 peppercorns, bruised
3 cloves
1 teaspoon mixed herbs
1 small chili, chopped
pinch of spice
pinch of ginger
½ teaspoon salt
¼ cup vinegar
2 tablespoons lemon juice
chopped parsley
lemon wedges

Wash, dry and trim fish fillets and arrange in a shallow, ovenproof casserole, add all ingredients except parsley and lemon wedges. Cover tightly with foil and cook in a moderate oven for 10–12 minutes. Remove dish from oven and allow to cool. Lift fish out on to a serving dish, strain liquid over and chill. Serve sprinkled with parsley and garnished with lemon wedges.

Coleslaw Special

Serves: 6

½ head savoy cabbage
1 large carrot
½ cup (125 ml) mayonnaise
4 tablespoons salad oil
1 tablespoon white vinegar
salt and pepper
¾ cup almonds
½ teaspoon caraway seeds (optional)

Shred the cabbage finely and place in a large lidded bowl. Grate the carrot and add to the cabbage and toss. In a bowl combine mayonnaise, oil, vinegar, salt and pepper and mix well, then pour over the salad and toss. Sliver the almonds and add to the salad with caraway seeds. Cover and chill for at least 1 hour, shaking bowl occasionally to mix. Toss well at serving.

Barbecued Sweet and Sour Spareribs

Serves: 4
Cooking time: 25–30 minutes
Barbecue on the grid over medium coals

8–10 pork spareribs
Crunchy Coleslaw — see recipe page 39
Saffron Rice Salad — see recipe page 85

Sweet and Sour Sauce:
2 tablespoons oil
2 cloves garlic, crushed
1 medium onion, finely chopped
1 tablespoon tomato catsup
2 tablespoons lemon juice
¼ teaspoon dried sage
3 tablespoons brown sugar, firmly packed
½ cup (125 ml) beef cube stock
2 teaspoons Worcestershire sauce
2 teaspoons French mustard
salt and pepper

Make sauce first by heating oil in a heavy pan on the barbecue, add garlic and onion and cook until soft. Add catsup, lemon juice, sage, brown sugar, stock, Worcestershire sauce, mustard, salt and pepper and heat, stirring until smooth and hot.
Add the spareribs to the pan and turn to coat well with the sauce, then place ribs on the grid over medium coals and cook for 18–20 minutes, until tender, turning and basting frequently with the sauce. Serve hot with coleslaw and saffron rice.

Lamb Chops in Rosemary Marinade

Serves: 4
Cooking time: 12–15 minutes
Barbecue on the grid over medium hot coals

8 lamb chops 1" (2½ cm) thick
Saffron Rice Salad — see recipe page 85
Tomato and Sour Cream Salad — see recipe
    page 38

Marinade:
3 tablespoons oil
2 tablespoons lemon juice
1 clove garlic, crushed
2 teaspoons rosemary
salt and pepper

Combine oil, lemon juice, garlic, rosemary, salt and pepper in a jar, cover and shake well to mix. Arrange chops in one layer in a shallow glass or enamel dish, pour marinade over the meat, baste and set aside in a cool place to marinate for 3–3½ hours, basting occasionally. Lift out chops and place on the grid over medium hot coals and cook for 12–15 minutes, until tender, turning often and basting with the marinade. Delicious served with suggested salads, crunchy French bread and chilled white wine.

Celery and Ginger Salad

Serves: 4

4 stalks of white celery
¼ lb (125 g) chopped mixed nuts
2 tablespoons chopped preserved ginger
2 tablespoons ginger syrup
½ cup (125 ml) French Dressing — see recipe
    page 92
1 tablespoon mayonnaise
4 crisp lettuce leaves

Chop the celery finely and place in a salad bowl with mixed nuts and preserved ginger. Combine ginger syrup with dressing and mayonnaise in a bowl and mix well, then spoon over the salad, toss and chill.
Arrange lettuce leaves on a serving plate, add salad, sprinkle with parsley and serve.

Sweet and Sour Appetisers

Serves: 4
Cooking time: 12–15 minutes
Barbecue on skewers over medium hot coals

1 lb (500 g) thick ham steaks
½ pineapple, peeled and cored
3 medium, firm tomatoes
½ (125 ml) Sweet and Sour Baste — see recipe
    page 88

Cut the ham into cubes; pineapple into pieces; tomatoes into chunks, and prepare the baste. Thread ham cubes, pineapple pieces and tomato chunks, alternately, on bamboo skewers. Brush with baste and cook over medium hot coals for 12–15 minutes, turning often, and basting. Remove from heat, baste and serve.

▲ RICE SALAD WITH STUFFED EGGS (RECIPE PAGE 76)

▲ BARBECUED FISH STEAKS WITH CAPERS (RECIPE PAGE 76)

Frankfurters with Cheese and Bacon

Serves: 4–6
Cooking time: 18–20 minutes
Barbecue on grid over medium hot coals

1½ lbs (750 g) thick, short frankfurters
water
prepared mustard
catsup
8 thick slices processed cheese
½ lb (250 g) bacon strips
bread rolls or buns

Place frankfurters in a pan, cover with water, bring to the boil and simmer 2–3 minutes, drain and cool. Split frankfurters almost through, spread inside with mustard and catsup, add cheese slices and close. Wrap each frankfurter with a strip of bacon and fasten with a tooth pick. Place on the grid over medium hot coals and cook for 12–15 minutes, turning often, until cheese starts to melt and bacon is crisp and golden. Serve with crunchy bread rolls or buns.

Barbecued Fish Steaks with Capers

Serves: 6
Cooking time: 12−15 minutes
Barbecue on the grid over medium coals

6 fish steaks
3 tablespoons lemon juice
3 tablespoons capers
3 scallions, finely chopped
1 tablespoon chopped chives
salt and pepper
Basic Lemon Baste — see recipe page 88
Cole Slaw Special — see recipe page 72

Arrange fish steaks in a shallow dish and sprinkle with lemon juice, capers, scallions, chives, salt and pepper and let stand for 30 minutes. Place fish on the grid over medium coals and cook for 12−15 minutes, until white and tender, turning twice. Brush with lemon baste in last few minutes of cooking. Serve with tartare sauce and cole slaw. *(Illustrated on page 74.)*

Rice Salad with Stuffed Eggs

Serves: 4−6
Cooking time: 15−18 minutes

½ cup rice
boiling salted water
1 medium red bell pepper, seeded and chopped
4−5 spring onions, chopped
1 teaspoon chervil
1 tablespoon finely chopped parsley
½ cup (125 ml) mayonnaise
salt and seasoned pepper
2 hard boiled eggs, shelled
4−5 lettuce leaves
black olives
garlic sausage slices
Old Fashioned Bread — see recipe page 85

Place rice in a pan and cover with boiling salted water. Bring back to the boil, reduce heat, cover and simmer for 15 minutes. Drain rice and rinse under cold water and drain again, then turn rice into a lidded plastic bowl and add bell pepper and spring onion. In a bowl combine chervil, parsley, ¾ of the mayonnaise, salt and seasoned pepper and mix well. Pour half this mixture over the rice and mix well; cover and chill.

Slice eggs in half, remove yolks and mash, then mix with remaining mayonnaise; spoon mixture back into egg white halves and chill. Arrange lettuce leaves in a bowl, add rice salad, top with stuffed eggs, black olives and arrange slices of sausage around edge. Serve with hot bread. *(Illustrated on page 74.)*

Barbecued Sirloin with Beer Sauce

Serves: 6
Cooking time: 15−18 minutes
Barbecue on the grid over hot coals

6 thick sirloin steaks, trimmed
Stuffed Tomatoes — see recipe page 14
lettuce salad with dressing

Beer Sauce:
1 small onion, minced
2 teaspoons prepared mustard
1 clove garlic, crushed
salt and seasoned pepper
3 tablespoons soy sauce
3 tablespoons oil
⅓ cup (85 ml) beer

Combine onion, mustard, garlic, salt, seasoned pepper, soy sauce and oil in a bowl and mix well, then stir in beer until smooth, for the sauce. Brush steaks liberally with the sauce, on both sides and place on the grid over hot coals. Cook for 6−8 minutes on each side, for rare, basting occasionally with the sauce and turning. Serve steak with stuffed tomatoes, crisp lettuce salad, hot French bread and chilled beer.

Zucchini Salad

Serves: 4–6

¾ lb (375 g) zucchini
4 stalks white celery
2 small carrots
2 scallions
1 tablespoon chopped parsley
salt and seasoned pepper
6 tablespoons mayonnaise
4 tablespoons lemon juice
4–6 crisp lettuce leaves

Thinly slice zucchini, celery, carrots and scallions and place in a salad bowl. Sprinkle with parsley, salt and seasoned pepper. Mix mayonnaise and lemon juice in a small bowl until smooth, then pour over the salad. Toss gently until all vegetables are coated. Serve salad on individual lettuce leaves.

Barbecued Chicken Italian Style

Serves: 4
Cooking time: 30–35 minutes
Barbecue on grid over medium hot coals

3 lbs (1½ kg) 4 chicken halves
4 tablespoons oil
1½ lbs (750 g) tomatoes, peeled and chopped
1 clove garlic crushed
1 teaspoon ground bay leaves
½ teaspoon thyme
¼ teaspoon oregano
salt and pepper
3 tablespoons grated Parmesan cheese
Crunchy Coleslaw — see recipe page 39
Saffron Rice Salad — see recipe page 85

In a heavy pan place oil and heat over coals, add tomatoes, garlic, ground bay leaves, thyme, oregano, salt and pepper and cook, stirring and mashing, until tomatoes are puréed. Fold in cheese and cook, stirring, for 2–3 minutes, then set pan aside.

Brush chicken halves generously with tomato and cheese sauce, on all sides. Place chicken on a grid over medium hot coals and cook for 30–35 minutes, basting with the sauce and turning two or three times. Serve with coleslaw and rice salad. (Illustrated on page 79.)

Stuffed Lettuce

Serves: 4
Cooking time: 35–40 minutes
Barbecue in casserole in hot ashes

4 large lettuce leaves
½ lb (250 g) pork sausage meat
2 tablespoons finely chopped green bell pepper
½ cup soft breadcrumbs
½ teaspoon marjoram
½ teaspoon chopped chives
½ teaspoon thyme
1 tablespoon chopped parsley
salt and pepper
1 egg, lightly beaten
1 tablespoon milk
½ cup catsup
¼ cup white wine
3 tablespoons butter

Wash and dry the lettuce leaves and set aside. Combine the pork sausage in a bowl with bell pepper, breadcrumbs, marjoram, chives, thyme, parsley, salt, pepper, egg and milk and mix well. Divide the mixture onto the lettuce leaves and roll up, tucking in ends neatly, and fasten with toothpicks. Arrange in a flameproof casserole and add catsup and wine mixed together. Butter paper and place on the top. Cover tightly and place casserole in hot ashes to cook for 35–40 minutes. Renew hot ashes occasionally. Delicious with barbecued quail, chicken or pork.

▲

Skewered Red Wine Burgers

Serves: 4
Cooking time: 18−20 minutes
Barbecue on skewers over medium hot coals

1½ lbs (750 g) lean ground beef
1 large onion, finely chopped
1½ cups soft breadcrumbs
1 egg
½ teaspoon thyme
1 teaspoon ground bay leaves
½ cup (125 ml) red wine
salt and pepper
3 tablespoons oil

In a bowl combine meat with onion, breadcrumbs, egg, thyme, ground bay leaves, wine, salt and pepper and mix thoroughly. Shape mixture into 8 patties and chill for 35−40 minutes. Thread patties on metal skewes and brush liberally with oil. Place over medium hot coals and cook for 18−20 minutes, turning often and basting with oil.

Barbecued Pork Spareribs

Serves: 4−6
Cooking time: 30 minutes
Barbecue on the grid over medium coals

8−10 pork spareribs
4 tablespoons oil
1 medium onion, chopped finely
1 tablespoon chopped scallions
1 clove garlic, crushed
1 teaspoon dry mustard
3 tablespoons catsup
1 teaspoon Worcestershire sauce
3 tablespoons vinegar
salt and pepper
1 teaspoon thyme
4 tablespoons honey
Glazed Pineapple Rings — see recipe page 34

Heat the oil in a pan, add onion, scallions and garlic and sauté until golden. Stir in dry mustard until smooth, then catusup, Worcestershire sauce, vinegar, salt, pepper, thyme and honey and cook gently for 10 minutes, stirring constantly. Remove from heat, add spareribs and baste. Drain meat and place on the grid over medium coals and cook for 18−20 minutes until tender, turning often and basting with the sauce. Serve hot with glazed pineapple rings.

▼

BARBECUED CHICKEN ITALIAN STYLE (RECIPE PAGE 77) ▶

Green Bean and Onion Salad

Serves: 4–6
Cooking time: 8–10 minutes

1 lb (500 g) green beans
boiling salted water
2 medium white onions
1 tablespoon chopped parsley
½ cup (125 ml) olive or salad oil
3 tablespoons white vinegar
1 clove garlic, crushed
salt and pepper

Wash, trim, string the beans and cut in half. Cook in a pan of boiling salted water for 8–10 minutes, drain, cool, then chill for 30 minutes. Peel and thinly slice the onions into rings and with parsley, and place with the beans in a salad bowl. In a jar combine oil, vinegar, garlic, salt and pepper, cover and shake vigorously to mix to a creamy dressing, then pour over the salad and toss. Cover and chill at least 2 hours.

Picnic Menu

Serves: 4–6

2 lbs (1 kg) cooked prawns, shelled and
*   de-veined*
sprigs of parsley
1 bunch of crisp white celery
Chicken Stuffed Cabbage Leaves — see
*   recipe this page*
Celery Slaw — see recipe page 82
Bell Peppers Filled with Ham and Rice — see
*   recipe on opposite page*
Glazed Onions and Raisins — see recipe on
*   opposite page*
bowl of black olives
Seafood Saffron Rice — see recipe page 82
Eggplant and Tomato Salad — see recipe on
*   opposite page*
Garlic Mushroom Salad — see recipe this page
Red Bell Peppers in Garlic Oil — see recipe
*   page 30*

Wash prawns and chill, then place in a bowl with sprigs of parsley. Prepare, cook and chill the different recipes and chill the olives. Serve at the picnic with bread sticks or French bread and red wine.
(Illustrated on pages 2 & 3.)

Garlic Mushroom Salad

Serves: 4–6

1 lb (500 g) mushrooms
1 tablespoon lemon juice
¼ cup salad oil
1 teaspoon minced garlic
salt and pepper
1 tablespoon chopped parsley

Trim and slice the mushrooms and place in a bowl. In a jar combine lemon juice, oil, garlic, salt, pepper and parsley, cover and shake well to mix, then pour over the mushrooms and toss. Cover and chill for at least 1 hour.
(Illustrated on pages 2 & 3.)

Chicken Stuffed Cabbage Leaves

Serves: 4–6
Cooking time: 40–45 minutes
Oven: 180°C 350°F

½ lb (250 g) cooked chicken, ground
6 large cabbage leaves
boiling water
1 tablespoon oil
1 large onion, finely chopped
1 clove garlic, crushed
1 small red bell pepper, seeded and finely
*   chopped*
1 cup cooked rice
1 tablespoon tomato catsup
¼ cup water
1 tablespoon chopped parsley
salt and pepper
½ cup (125 ml) white wine

Trim cabbage leaves, remove stems and blanch in a pan of boiling water for 3–4 minutes; drain well and allow to cool. Heat oil in a pan, add onion and garlic and sauté until soft, add bell pepper and cook, stirring for 3–4 minutes. Spoon into a bowl and add rice, tomato catsup and water, mixed together, then add chicken, parsley, salt and pepper, and mix well.

Spread cabbage leaves, divide mixture evenly onto the leaves and wrap, tucking in ends neatly. Place in a greased ovenproof casserole dish and sprinkle with wine. Cover and cook in a moderate oven for 15 minutes, uncover and cook a further 10–15 minutes until lightly browned. Remove dish from oven and allow to cool, then chill.
(Illustrated on pages 2 & 3.)

Bell Peppers Filled with Ham and Rice

Serves: 4–6
Cooking time: 30–35 minutes
Oven: 180°C   350°F

6 medium green bell peppers
boiling salted water
3 tablespoons butter
1 medium onion, finely chopped
¼ lb (125 g) mushrooms, chopped
¼ lb (125 g) ham, finely chopped
1 cup cooked rice
salt and seasoned pepper
1 teaspoon mixed herbs
¼ cup white wine
1 tablespoon oil

Cut a slice from the stalk end of each bell pepper, remove seeds, place in a pan of boiling salted water and simmer for 15 minutes. Remove peppers from the pan, drain and cool.

Meanwhile, melt butter in a pan, add onion and sauté until soft, add mushrooms and cook for 3–4 minutes, stirring. Remove from heat and add ham, rice, salt, seasoned pepper, herbs and wine and mix well. Fill peppers with this mixture and arrange in a greased baking dish, brush with oil and cook in a moderate oven for 15–20 minutes. Lift out peppers, cool and chill, or serve hot.
(Illustrated on pages 2 & 3.)

Eggplant and Tomato Salad

Serves: 4–6
Cooking time: 5–6 minutes

2 eggplants
boiling salted water
2 large tomatoes
salt and seasoned pepper
2 tablespoons lemon juice
1 tablespoon salad oil
1 tablespoon chopped parsley

Lower eggplants into a pan of boiling, salted water and simmer for 5–6 minutes. Drain, then rinse in cold water to cool. Peel and slice the eggplant; peel and chop the tomatoes and place in a salad bowl. In a jar combine salt, seasoned pepper, lemon juice, oil and parsley, cover and shake well to mix, then pour over the eggplant. Cover and chill.
(Illustrated on pages 2 & 3.)

Glazed Onions and Raisins

Serves: 4–6
Cooking time: 25–30 minutes

12 pearl onions
boiling water
4 tablespoons butter
1 tablespoon sugar
salt and pepper
1 tablespoon raisins
2 tablespoons olive oil

Peel onions and drop into a pan of boiling water, to blanch, for 6–7 minutes, drain well. Melt butter in a pan, add sugar, salt, pepper, onions and raisins. Cover and cook gently for 12–15 minutes, shaking pan and stirring occasionally, until onions are tender and well glazed. Remove onions and raisins and place in a bowl, sprinkle with oil, toss and chill.
(Illustrated on pages 2 & 3.)

Seafood Saffron Rice

Serves: 4–6
Cooking time: 40–45 minutes

> ½ lb (250 g) cooked shelled mussels
> 7 oz (220 g) can crabmeat, drained
> 1 cup rice
> ½ lb (125 g) shelled peas
> 4 tablespoons oil
> 1 medium onion, chopped
> 1 clove garlic, crushed
> 2 medium tomatoes, chopped
> ½ teaspoon saffron
> salt and pepper
> chopped parsley

Cook rice in a pan of boiling salted water for 15 minutes, drain, wash and cool. Meanwhile cook peas in boiling salted water for 10–12 minutes and drain. Heat oil in a pan, add onion and garlic and sauté until soft, add tomatoes and cook 6–7 minutes, stirring occasionally. Stir in saffron, salt, pepper, rice, peas, mussels and crabmeat, cover and cook gently for 15–18 minutes to heat through. Sprinkle with parsley and stir. Spoon into a salad bowl, cool, then chill.
(Illustrated on pages 2 & 3.)

Celery Slaw

Serves: 4–6

> 5 stalks celery
> 1 teaspoon salt
> 3 teaspoons sugar
> ½ teaspoon ground ginger
> pinch of pepper
> 4 tablespoons white vinegar
> ½ cup (125 ml) salad oil
> ½ cup (125 ml) sour cream

Slice the celery finely and place in a salad bowl. In a jar combine salt, sugar, ginger, pepper, vinegar and oil, cover and shake well to mix. Stir in sour cream until well blended. Pour the dressing over the celery and toss, cover and chill for 2 hours.
(Illustrated on pages 2 & 3.)

Mediterranean Lamb Kebabs

Serves: 6
Cooking time: 18–20 minutes
Barbecue on skewers over hot coals

> 2 lbs (1 kg) lean lamb, cubed
> ½ cup (125 ml) oil
> ½ cup (125 ml) white wine
> 1 tablespoon lemon juice
> 1 teaspoon oregano
> 1 clove garlic, crushed
> 1 teaspoon ground bay leaves
> salt and pepper
> 1 green bell pepper, seeded
> 3 medium onions, quartered
> Continental Potato Salad — see recipe page 38
> Green Bean and Onion Salad — see
>   recipe page 80

Place the lamb in a glass or enamel dish. In a jar combine oil, wine, lemon juice, oregano, garlic, ground bay leaves, salt and pepper, cover and shake well, then pour over the lamb. Cover the dish and set aside in a cool place to marinate for 2–2½ hours, basting occasionally. Cut bell pepper into large chunks. Lift out lamb and drain, then thread on to skewers, alternating with pepper chunks and onion quarters. Barbecue over hot coals for 18–20 minutes, turning frequently, until meat is tender, basting often with the marinade. Serve hot with potato salad, green bean salad and hot French bread.

Barbecued Grapefruit

Serves: 6
Cooking time: 20–25 minutes
Barbecue on the grid over hot coals

> 3 large grapefruit
> ⅓ cup brown sugar, firmly packed
> 3 tablespoons butter
> ½ cup (125 ml) rum, warmed

Cut grapefruit in half, loosen the flesh from the skin and cut into segments. Sprinkle brown sugar over the halves and dot with butter. Place fruit on the grid over hot coals, flesh side up, and cook for 20–25 minutes, until heated through. Sprinkle warmed rum over the grapefruit, ignite and serve for dessert.

Spicy Leg of Lamb

Serves: 6–8
Cooking time: 2–2¼ hours
Barbecue on the spit over medium hot coals

4 lbs (2 kg) boned leg of lamb
1 cup soft breadcrumbs
1 small onion, finely chopped
1 teaspoon chopped rosemary
1 teaspoon mixed herbs
1 teaspoon chopped parsley
¼ cup (65 ml) white wine or water
2 cloves garlic, slivered
salt and pepper
6–8 Foil Wrapped Potatoes — see
 recipe page 43
Tangy Eggplant — see recipe page 48

Spicy Sauce:
4 tablespoons chutney
1 tablespoon Worcestershire sauce
1 tablespoon soy sauce
1 tablespoon catsup
3 tablespoons red wine
2 tablespoons oil
pinch of cayenne pepper
1 tablespoon brown sugar

Combine breadcrumbs, onion, rosemary, mixed herbs, parsley, and wine in a bowl and mix well, then place mixture in the meat, roll and tie securely with white string. Insert spit rod lengthways through the center of the meat and secure, spike with garlic, sprinkle with salt and pepper and place on the spit over medium hot coals. Cook for 2–2½ hours, until tender.
Meanwhile, combine all ingredients for sauce in a pan, mix well, and set on the side of the barbecue to warm. In last ½ hour of cooking, baste the meat often with the sauce. Lift lamb from the spit onto a carving tray, remove rod and allow meat to rest for 4–5 minutes, then slice. Serve with remaining sauce, potatoes and eggplant.

Marinated Venison on the Spit

Serves: 6–8
Cooking time: 1–1¼ hours
Barbecue on the spit over medium hot coals

4 lbs (2 kg) boned loin of venison
4 tablespoons butter, melted
½ cup (125 ml) heavy cream
6–8 Foil Wrapped Potatoes — see
 recipe page 43
red currant jelly

Marinade:
1 large onion, coarsley chopped
2 medium carrots, sliced
¼ teaspoon thyme
1 tablespoon chopped parsley
1 clove garlic, crushed
4–5 peppercorns, bruised
3 tablespoons olive oil
½ cup (125 ml) wine vinegar
2 cups (500 ml) burgundy or red wine

Roll the venison, tie with string and place in a glass dish. Place onion and carrots around the meat. Combine the ingredients for the marinade, mix well and pour over the meat and vegetables. Cover and set aside to marinate for 8 hours or overnight, basting occasionally. Lift out the meat, pat dry and thread, through the center of the flesh, onto the spit rod. Strain marinade into a pan and reserve. Place rod on the spit over medium hot coals and cook for 1–1¼ hours, until tender, basting alternately with melted butter and marinade, while cooking.
Meanwhile cook foil wrapped potatoes. Remove meat and place on a carving board and let rest for 8–10 minutes. Boil marinade to reduce to 1 cup, remove from heat and fold in the cream for the gravy.
Remove the string, slice the venison and serve with the gravy and red currant jelly, foil wrapped potatoes and tossed salad.

Marinated Beef Kebabs

Serves: 4
Cooking time: 8–10 minutes
Barbecue on skewers over hot coals

1½ lbs (750 g) thick barbecue steak
2 medium onions, cut in wedges
Foil Wrapped Potatoes — see recipe page 43
Goddess Salad — see recipe page 54

Marinade:
1 clove garlic, crushed
salt and pepper
1 teaspoon honey
1 tablespoon soy sauce
1 tablespoon dry sherry
2 tablespoons salad oil

Trim fat from meat, cut into 1″ (2½ cm) cubes and place in a bowl. Combine garlic, salt, pepper, honey, soy sauce, sherry and oil in a bowl and mix until smooth, then pour over the meat and marinate for at least 1 hour. Drain meat and thread on skewers, alternately, with onion wedges. Place over hot coals and cook for 8–10 minutes, basting with the marinade. Serve kebabs with potatoes and salad.

Scallop Kebabs

Serves: 4
Cooking time: 15–18 minutes
Barbecue on skewers over hot coals

16 scallops
8 strips of bacon, cut in pieces
16 button mushrooms
8 small onions, cut in halves
lemon wedges for garnish

Marinade:
1 clove garlic, crushed
2 tablespoons oil
1 tablespoon lemon juice
1 tablespoon dry sherry
½ teaspoon marjoram
salt and pepper

For the marinade, combine garlic, oil, lemon juice, sherry, marjoram, salt and pepper in a jar, cover and shake well until smooth.
Wrap scallops individually in bacon pieces, then thread on skewers, alternately, with mushrooms and onion halves. Lay the kebabs in a shallow dish, pour marinade over them and allow to stand for 30 minutes, turning kebabs occasionally and basting. Lift out kebabs, place on the barbecue over hot coals and cook for 15–20 minutes, turning and basting with marinade often. Garnish with lemon wedges.

Pork on the Spit with Skewered Onions and Tomatoes

Serves: 6
Cooking time: 2–2¼ hours
Barbecue on the spit over medium coals

4 lbs (2 kg) rolled loin of pork, scored
salt
12 medium onions, peeled and parboiled
6 medium tomatoes
oil
6 Baked Potatoes — see recipe page 29

Thread loin of pork on a spit rod. For good crackling, rub salt generously into the skin. Place rod on the spit over medium coals and cook for 2–2¼ hours, until meat is tender and crackling is golden brown.
Meanwhile, prepare and cook potatoes in ashes for 1 hour. Thread onions and tomatoes on separate skewers, brush with oil and cook on the grid over medium coals for 8–10 minutes, turning often and brushing with oil while cooking.
Remove pork from the spit and let stand 5 minutes. Remove string, carve and serve with baked potatoes, skewered onions and tomatoes, garlic bread and dry white wine.

Saffron Rice

Serves: 4
Cooking time: 30–35 minutes
Barbecue in a casserole over medium coals

1 cup rice
4 tablespoons butter
1 clove garlic, crushed
½ teaspoon saffron
salt and pepper
1 tablespoon chopped parsley
2 cups (500 ml) chicken stock
½ cup (125 ml) white wine

Heat butter in a flameproof casserole, add rice and garlic and stir. Cook until rice begins to color. Remove from heat and stir in saffron, salt, pepper, parsley, stock and wine. Cover and cook over medium coals for 25–30 minutes, until moisture is absorbed and rice is tender. Serve hot with barbecued poultry, or chilled.

Fennel and Lemon Salad

Serves: 4

1 bunch of fennel
grated rind from ½ lemon
flesh of 1 lemon, chopped
2 tablespoons chopped parsley

Creamy Dressing:
3 tablespoons olive oil
1 tablespoon lemon juice
2 teaspoons sugar
salt and pepper
2 tablespoons cream

Slice the fennel leaves finely and place in a salad bowl with lemon rind and flesh and parsley. Combine oil in a jar with lemon juice, sugar, salt and pepper, cover and shake to mix. Stir in cream until blended, then pour over the salad. Toss well and chill for 1 hour. Delicious with barbecued fish or poultry.

Old Fashioned Bread

Serves: 4–6
Cooking time: 25–30 minutes
Oven: 220°C reduce to 180°C
        425°F reduce to 350°F

4 cups flour
1½ tablespoons baking powder
1 teaspoon salt
6 tablespoons lard or butter, softened
1½ cups (375 ml) sour or fresh milk

Sift flour, baking powder and salt into a bowl and rub in lard or butter with the fingertips until mixture is like fine breadcrumbs. Make a well in the center and pour in milk. Using a knife, cut the mixture into dough, then turn out on to a floured board and lightly knead. Shape into a round and place on a greased baking tray. Cut top of dough with deep slits in a cross, brush with a little extra milk and sprinkle with flour. Cook in a hot oven for 10–12 minutes, until golden, reduce heat to moderate and cook a further 15–18 minutes. Serve hot with lots of butter or margarine.

Garlic Bread

Serves: 4–6
Cooking time: 18–20 minutes
Barbecued in foil over medium coals

2 loaves French bread
½ cup (125 g) butter, softened
2–3 cloves garlic, crushed
1 teaspoon finely chopped parsley
salt and pepper

In a bowl combine butter, garlic, parsley, salt and pepper and mix well until creamy. Cut French bread partly through, into 1″ (2½ cm) slices, diagonally. Spread garlic butter between the slices and press together. Wrap each loaf in doubled aluminium foil and seal. Place on the grid over medium coals for 18–20 minutes to heat through. Cut through slices and serve hot.

Garlic Butter

½ cup (125 g) butter, softened
2–3 cloves garlic, crushed
1 teaspoon finely chopped parsley
salt and pepper

In a bowl combine butter, garlic, parsley, salt and pepper and mix well. Spoon into a small container to fill, cover, and chill. Use for garlic bread or to brush over kebabs.

Mustard Butter

½ cup (125 g) butter, softened
2 teaspoons lemon juice
2 teaspoons finely chopped parsley
1 teaspoon prepared mustard
salt and pepper

In a bowl combine butter, lemon juice, parsley, mustard, salt and pepper and mix well. Spoon into a small container to fill, cover, and chill. Use on barbecued steaks or hamburgers.

Fine Herb Butter

½ cup (125 g) butter, softened
1 tablespoon finely chopped parsley
1 tablespoon finely chopped chives
½ teaspoon tarragon
½ teaspoon chervil
salt and pepper

In a bowl combine butter, parsley, chives, tarragon, chervil, salt and pepper and mix well. Pat into a rectangular shape, wrap and chill. Cut into slices and add to barbecue steaks or hamburgers for a piquant flavor.

Anchovy Butter

½ cup (125 g) butter, softened
2 teaspoons anchovy paste
1 tablespoon finely chopped parsley

Combine butter in a bowl with anchovy paste and parsley and mix well. Spoon into a small container to fill, cover, and chill. Use to brush the cavity and over fish, or use in place of garlic butter on bread.

Dill Butter

2 hard boiled eggs, yolks only
½ cup (125 g) butter, softened
4 teaspoons of dill
salt and pepper

Press yolks of eggs through a sieve into a bowl, combine with butter, dill, salt and pepper and mix well. Pat mixture into a rectangular shape, wrap and chill. Use on trout or any seafood.

Herb Marinade for Lamb

½ cup (125 ml) salad oil
1 small onion, finely chopped
1 clove garlic, crushed
1 teaspoon thyme
1 teaspoon marjoram
1 teaspoon salt
dash of seasoned pepper
3 tablespoons chopped parsley
3 tablespoons lemon juice

Combine all ingredients in a jar, cover and shake vigorously until mixed and smooth. Place lamb in a glass dish and pour marinade over, baste and chill for 1½–2 hours, basting occasionally. Baste lamb with the marinade while cooking. Makes a little over ¾ cup of marinade.

Herb and Wine Marinade for Poultry

Cooking time: 6–7 minutes

1 cup (250 ml) dry white wi...
3 tablespoons lemon j...
1 tablespoon whi...
2 cloves garl...
1 teaspo...
2 tablespo...
salt and pep...

In a pan combine w...
tarragon, oil, salt and...
simmering. Cover and...
flavors to blend. Pour...
Makes 1½ cups of marina...

All Purpose Ma...

½ cup (125 ml) olive or salad oil
½ cup (125 ml) dry sherry
3 tablespoons soy sauce
1 teaspoon Worcestershire Sauce
2 cloves garlic, crushed
salt and pepper

In a jar or blender combine oil, sherry, soy a...
Worcestershire sauces, garlic, salt and pepper...
cover and shake well or blend, until smooth. Pour...
over meats, seafood or poultry. Roasts should
marinate for at least 24 hours, steaks for 4 hours,
seafood and poultry for 1–2 hours. Makes a little
over 1¼ cups of marinade.

Red Wine Marinade for Pork

Cooking time: 6–7 minutes

1 cup (250 ml) dry red wine
2 tablespoons tarragon vinegar
2 cloves garlic, crushed
2 tablespoons olive oil
1 teaspoon dried basil
salt and pepper

In a pan combine wine, vinegar, garlic, oil, basil,
salt and pepper and cook gently until simmering.
Cover and set aside for 1 hour to allow flavors to
blend. Pour over pork to marinate. Makes a little
over 1¼ cups of marinade.

Honey Marinade for Chicken

2 tablespoons white wine
1 teaspoon dry mustard
1 teaspoon rosemary
2 tablespoons honey
1 teaspoon Worcestershire sauce
dash of Tabasco sauce
2 tablespoons lemon juice
½ cup (125 ml) olive or salad oil

...mix mustard with wine until smooth, stir in
...honey, Worcestershire and Tabasco
...on juice and oil. Cover and shake until
...d smooth. Pour over chicken in a
...ste, and marinade in the refrigerator
...turning chicken and basting occa-
...hicken with the marinade while
...cup of marinade.

...Wine
...Lamb

Co...tes

½ c... ...) dry white wine
1 tab... ...on tarragon vinegar
1 clove garlic, crushed
1 tablespoon olive oil
2 tablespoons honey
1 teaspoon chopped mint
salt and pepper

In a pan combine wine, vinegar, garlic, oil, honey,
mint, salt and pepper and cook gently until simmering. Cover and set aside for 1 hour to allow flavors
to blend. Pour over lamb to marinate. Makes a little
over ¾ cup of marinade.

Designed by Michele Emblem
731700
ATHENA
© Athena International
Printed in England

Pineapple Marinade for Steak

1 cup (250 ml) pineapple juice
3 tablespoons oil
1 clove garlic, crushed
salt and seasoned pepper
3 tablespoons brown sugar
1 tablespoon soy sauce

Combine all ingredients in a jar, cover and shake vigorously until fully mixed. Pour over steak in a glass dish and marinate for 3–3½ hours, basting occasionally. Brush meat with marinade while cooking. Makes a little over 1¼ cups of marinade.

Soy and Ginger Marinade

2 tablespoons olive oil
4 tablespoons soy sauce
2 tablespoons firmly packed brown sugar
2 tablespoons red wine
1 teaspoon grated, fresh ginger
1 clove garlic, crushed
salt and pepper

In a jar combine oil, soy sauce, brown sugar, wine, ginger, garlic, salt and pepper, cover and shake vigorously to mix well. Pour over meats, poultry or seafood to marinate. Makes a little over ⅔ cup of marinade.

Teriyaki Marinade

⅓ cup (85 ml) dry sherry
½ cup (125 ml) soy sauce
⅓ cup (85 ml) pineapple juice
1 tablespoon firmly packed brown sugar
1 small onion, chopped
1 clove garlic, crushed
salt and pepper
½ teaspoon ground ginger

In a blender combine sherry, soy sauce, pineapple juice, brown sugar, onion, garlic, ginger, salt and pepper, cover and blend until smooth. Pour over meat to marinate. Makes about 1¼ cups of marinade.

Basic Lemon Baste

½ cup (125 g) butter, melted
3 tablespoons lemon juice
salt and pepper

Combine melted butter and lemon juice in a jar, season with salt and pepper, cover and shake well to mix. Brush generously over seafood or poultry during cooking time. Makes ¾ cup (185 ml) of baste.

Sweet and Sour Baste

Cooking time: 15 minutes

15 oz (450 g) can crushed pineapple
1 cup (250 ml) dry white wine
1 tablespoon white vinegar
2 tablespoons salad oil
1 tablespoon soy sauce
1 medium white onion, minced
1 tablespoon firmly packed brown sugar
1 teaspoon lemon juice
1 clove garlic, crushed
salt and pepper

Combine all ingredients in a pan and bring to the boil, reduce heat and simmer gently for 10–12 minutes, stirring constantly. Brush generously on or fowl on the barbecue. Can also be used as a marinade. Makes 3⅓ cups.

Savoury Raisin Baste

Cooking time: 15 minutes

¼ lb (125 g) raisins, minced
1 medium onion, minced
1 clove garlic, minced
2 tablespoons tomato catsup
2 tablespoons white wine
1 tablespoon white vinegar
1 tablespoon firmly packed brown sugar
½ teaspoon prepared mustard
salt and pepper

Combine all ingredients in a pan, bring to the boil and simmer for 12–15 minutes. Brush generously on meats, fish or poultry. This baste becomes a crusty, sweet and sour glaze during cooking. Makes about 1 cup of baste.

Tarragon Baste

Cooking time: 5–6 minutes

½ cup (125 ml) tarragon vinegar
1 cup (250 g) firmly packed brown sugar
4 tablespoons butter

Combine all ingredients in a pan, bring to the boil and stir until sugar is dissolved. Allow to cool and use as a baste on lamb or pork. Makes 1¾ cups of baste.

Wine Vinegar Dressing

4 tablespoons white or red wine vinegar
salt and pepper
½ teaspoon dry mustard
½ teaspoon sugar
⅓ cup (165 ml) olive or salad oil

Place vinegar, salt, pepper, mustard and sugar in a blender and whirl for 2–3 minutes. Still blending add olive oil, a drop at a time, until fully absorbed and dressing is creamy. Makes almost 1 cup of dressing.

Thousand Island Dressing

¾ cup (185 ml) mayonnaise
6 stuffed olives
¼ of a small green bell pepper
2 gherkins
½ teaspoon salt
2 teaspoons chopped chives
½ cup (85 ml) catsup
1 hard boiled egg

Chop olives, pepper and gherkins finely. Place mayonnaise in a bowl and stir in olives, pepper, gherkins, salt, chives and catsup and mix well. Chop egg finely, fold into the mixture and chill. Makes about 1 cup of dressing.

Yogurt Coleslaw Dressing

1 cup (250 ml) Tangy Mayonnaise — see
  recipe page 91
4 tablespoons natural yogurt
½ teaspoon salt
1 teaspoon sugar

In a bowl combine mayonnaise, yogurt, salt and sugar and blend well together, then chill. Makes about 1¼ cups of dressing.

White Salad Cream

½ cup (125 ml) cream
2 teaspoons tarragon vinegar
salt and pepper
2 teaspoons lemon juice
2 egg whites

Whip the cream in a bowl, until stiff, then gradually stir in the vinegar and lemon juice, season with salt and pepper to taste. Beat the egg whites in a separate bowl until stiff, then fold into the cream mixture. Makes almost ¾ cup of salad cream.

Classic French Dressing

¾ cup (185 ml) olive oil
¼ cup white vinegar
1 clove garlic, crushed
salt and pepper

In a jar or blender combine oil, vinegar, garlic, salt and pepper, cover and shake vigorously or blend, until smooth and creamy. Chill for at least 30 minutes. Makes 1 cup of dressing.

Exotic Herb Dressing

½ cup (125 ml) olive oil
3 tablespoons white vinegar
1 clove garlic, crushed
1 tablespoon chopped parsley
½ teaspoon rosemary
½ teaspoon thyme
½ teaspoon basil
salt and pepper

In a blender combine oil, vinegar, garlic, parsley, rosemary, thyme, basil, salt and pepper, cover and blend until smooth and creamy. Chill for at least 30 minutes. Makes almost ¾ cup of dressing.

Coleslaw Dressing

1 cup (250 ml) mayonnaise
1 teaspoon dry mustard
1 teaspoon sugar
salt and pepper
4 tablespoons French Dressing — see recipe
 page 92
¼ cup (65 ml) heavy cream

In a bowl mix mustard, sugar, salt and pepper with a little French dressing until smooth, stir in remainder of dressing, then fold in mayonnaise and cream. Stir until thoroughly blended, then chill. Makes 1½ cups of dressing.

Green Mayonnaise

1 teaspoon lemon juice
salt and pepper
1 tablespoon chopped parsley
1 teaspoon chervil
1 teaspoon tarragon
1 cup (250 ml) mayonnaise

In a bowl mix together lemon juice, salt, pepper, parsley, chervil and tarragon and let stand for 5 minutes, then fold in mayonnaise and mix thoroughly until blended. Serve with seafood salad. Makes a little over 1 cup of mayonnaise.

Egg Mustard Dressing

3 egg yolks
½ teaspoon salt
2 teaspoons prepared mustard
1½ cups (375 ml) olive or salad oil
4 tablespoons lemon juice

Combine egg yolks, salt and mustard in a blender and whirl on 3 for 1–2 minutes. Still blending gradually add oil, drop at a time, until fully mixed, then gradually blend in lemon juice. Makes nearly 2 cups of dressing.

Mayonnaise

2 eggs
2 cups (500 ml) salad oil
6 tablespoons lemon juice
½ teaspoon salt
½ teaspoon dry mustard
pepper

Place eggs, ½ cup oil, lemon juice, salt, mustard and pepper in a blender and whirl, add remaining oil in a steady steam, until absorbed and creamy. Makes about 2¼ cups of mayonnaise.

Lemon Dressing

6 tablespoons lemon juice
1 teaspoon salt
1 teaspoon sugar
¼ teaspoon paprika
⅛ teaspoon pepper
1 tablespoon chopped parsley
2 teaspoons chopped chives
1 cup (250 ml) olive or salad oil

In a blender place lemon juice, salt, sugar, paprika and pepper and whirl 1–2 minutes. Add parsley and chives and blend 1–2 minutes. While still blending gradually pour in the oil and blend until mixed and creamy. Makes almost 1½ cups of dressing.

Spicy Island Dressing

½ cup (125 ml) mayonnaise
1 teaspoon chili sauce
1 tablespoon catsup
1 teaspoon Worcestershire sauce
dash of Tabasco sauce
½ teaspoon paprika
1 hard boiled egg, chopped
1 gherkin, chopped
salt and seasoned pepper
1 tablespoon chopped celery
1 tablespoon chives

Combine all ingredients in a blender and mix until smooth and creamy, then pour into bowl, cover and chill. Makes a little over ¾ cup.

Mustard Mayonnaise

½ cup (125 ml) mayonnaise
2 tablespoons French mustard
½ teaspoon tumeric

Combine mayonnaise, mustard and turmeric in a bowl and mix thoroughly until smooth, then chill. Makes ⅔ cup.

Italian Dressing

½ teaspoon dry mustard
4 tablespoons red wine vinegar
½ teaspoon fresh basil, chopped finely
salt and pepper
1 teaspoon anchovy sauce
½ cup (125 ml) olive or salad oil

Mix mustard in a jar with a little vinegar until smooth, add basil, salt, pepper, anchovy sauce and remaining vinegar, cover and shake well. Add oil, cover and shake vigorously until mixture is creamy. Makes about ¾ cup of dressing.

Vinaigrette Dressing

1 teaspoon dry mustard
¼ cup white vinegar
½ teaspoon salt
1 teaspoon chopped chervil
1 teaspoon chopped chives
1 teaspoon chopped tarragon
1 teaspoon chopped parsley
¾ cup (185 ml) olive or salad oil

In a jar mix mustard with a little vinegar until smooth, gradually stir in remainder of vinegar with the salt and swirl. Add chervil, chives, tarragon, parsley and oil, cover and shake vigorously to mix well until creamy. This dressing can be made in a blender. Makes a little over 1 cup of dressing.

Tangy Mayonnaise

13 oz (400 g) can sweetened condensed milk
1 teaspoon salt
1 teaspoon dry mustard
¾ cup (185 ml) white vinegar
3 tablespoons cream

In a bowl mix salt and mustard with a little vinegar until smooth, gradually stir in remaining vinegar, condensed milk and cream and mix until fully blended, then chill. Makes almost 2 cups of mayonnaise.

Blender Mayonnaise

3 large egg yolks
½ teaspoon of salt
dash of white pepper
pinch of cayenne pepper
1 teaspoon sugar
1 teaspoon French mustard
3−4 drops lemon juice
2½ cups (625 ml) olive or salad oil
6 tablespoons white vinegar

All ingredients should be at room temperature. Combine egg yolks, salt, white and cayenne pepper, sugar, mustard and lemon juice in a blender. Turn to medium speed and blend for 2−3 minutes. Gradually add 4 tablespoons of oil, 2−3 drops at a time, through lid insert hole, until mixture has thickened. Add the vinegar slowly and, still blending, add remainder of the oil in a steady stream and blend for 1−2 minutes. Do not run above medium speed, as high speed causes air pockets to form and upsets smooth blending. Makes about 3 cups.

Cheese Dressing

¾ cup (185 ml) olive or salad oil
¼ cup white vinegar
8 tablespoons crumbled roquefort cheese
salt and pepper

In a bowl combine oil, vinegar, cheese, salt and pepper and mix thoroughly until smooth. Chill for at least 30 minutes. Makes a little over 1¼ cups of dressing.

Blue Cheese Dressing

¼ lb (125 g) blue cheese
½ cup (125 ml) olive or salad oil
¼ teaspoon paprika
½ teaspoon dry mustard
1 tablespoon lemon juice
1 tablespoon white vinegar
1 teaspoon Worcestershire sauce
2 teaspoons brandy
salt to taste

Rub cheese through a sieve into a bowl and gradually mix in the oil. Combine paprika and mustard with lemon juice until smooth, then stir into the cheese and oil, with vinegar, brandy and salt. Mix thoroughly until smooth and creamy. Chill for at least 30 minutes. Makes 1½ cups of dressing.

Creamy French Dressing with Caraway Seeds

¾ cup (185 ml) olive or salad oil
¼ cup (65 ml) white wine vinegar
½ cup (125 ml) heavy cream
1 clove garlic, crushed
1 teaspoon caraway seeds
salt and black pepper

In a blender combine oil, vinegar, cream, garlic, caraway, salt and black pepper and blend until smooth and very creamy. Chill for at least 30 minutes. Makes 1½ cups of dressing.

French Dressing

½ teaspoon dry mustard
3 tablespoons white vinegar
pinch of salt
1 clove garlic, peeled and halved
dash of black pepper
1 small ice cube, approximately 2 teaspoons
½ cup (125 ml) olive or salad oil

In a jar mix mustard with a little vinegar until smooth. Add salt, garlic, pepper and remaining vinegar, cover and shake. Add ice cube and oil, cover and shake vigorously until cube has dissolved and mixture is creamy. Discard garlic before serving. Makes almost ¾ cup of dressing.

Liquid Measures Table

IMPERIAL	METRIC
1 teaspoon	5 ml
*1 tablespoon (Aust)	20 ml
2 fluid ounces (¼ cup)	65 ml
4 fluid ounces (½ cup)	125 ml
8 fluid ounces (1 cup)	250 ml
1 pint (20 fluid ounces = 2½ cups)	625 ml

USA	METRIC
*1 tablespoon (also UK and NZ)	15 ml
1 pint (16 ounces = 2 cups)	500 ml
All other measures same as	
for imperial, above	

*Tablespoon measures used in the recipes in this book are 15 ml.

Solid Measures Table

AVOIRDUPOIS	METRIC
1 ounce	30 g
4 ounces (¼ lb)	125 g
8 ounces (½ lb)	250 g
12 ounces (¾ lb)	375 g
16 ounces (1 lb)	500 g
24 ounces (1½ lb)	750 g
32 ounces (2 lb)	1000 g (1 kg)

Oven Temperature Table

DESCRIPTION	GAS		ELECTRIC		DIAL MARK
	C	F	C	F	
Cool	100	200	110	225	¼
Very slow	120	250	120	250	½
Slow	150	300	150	300	1–2
Moderately slow	160	325	170	340	3
Moderate	180	350	190	375	4
Moderately hot	190	375	220	425	5–6
Hot	200	400	250	475	6–7
Very hot	230	450	270	525	8–9

Index